The Meaning of the Names of Our Lord

presented by our Guide

Shaykh Muhammad Sa^{c}id al-Jamal ar-Rifa^{c}i ash-Shadhuli
Head of the Higher Sufi Council in Jerusalem
and the Holy Land
Teacher at the holy mosques at al-Aqsa in Jerusalem

بسم الله الرحمن الرحيم

bismi-llāhi-r-raḥmani-r-raḥīm

In the Name of Allāh, the Merciful, the Compassionate

Second Printing October, 2003
Cover art by Huda al-Jamal
ISBN 1-892595-15-X

Published by Sidi Muhammad Press
www.sufimaster.org
965 Quarry Street, Petaluma
CA 94954
(707) 765-0904

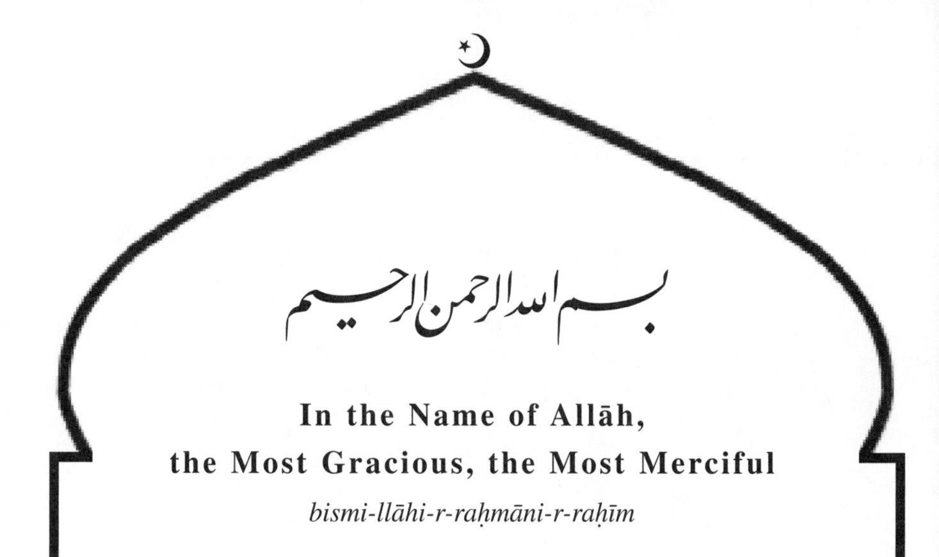

In the Name of Allāh,
the Most Gracious, the Most Merciful

bismi-llāhi-r-raḥmāni-r-raḥīm

Introduction

The names by which Allāh is known can be divided into categories. Traditionally the first two categories are the names of the essence (*adẖ-dẖat*), such as *Allāh* and *ar-Raḥmān*, and the names of the qualities (*aṣ-ṣafat*) such as *ar-Raḥīm* and *al-Bāriʾ*. And they can be divided further into names of the Mercy, and names of the Majesty. But the name Allāh called the Supreme Name stands alone. There is a *ḥadītẖ* which says, “To God belong ninety-nine names.” So that while any two lists add up to more than ninety-nine, any one list is limited to this number. The names are revealed directly in *al-Qurʾān*, or from the meaning given in certain passages, or they are names that are traditionally known, but are not in *al-Qurʾān*. Some names are found derived from the Arabic grammar of the names in *al-Qurʾān*, but they are not widely accepted, for example, *al-Gẖaffār* (page 24) from *al-Gẖafūr* (page 41).

الله الله الله

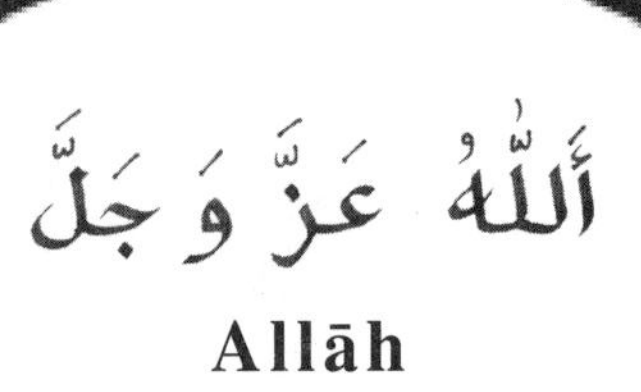

Allāh

Great and Almighty

This majestic vocal name Allāh is mentioned in the Holy Qur°ān two thousand, six hundred and ninety-seven different places. It is the Supreme Name.

Allāh brings the dead to life and shows you His signs. (2:73)

Believers are those who, when God is mentioned, feel a tremor in their hearts. (8:2)

Allāh chooses for His mercy whom He wills. And Allāh is the owner of Great Bounty. (2:105)

When Jesus became conscious of their disbelief, he cried, "Who will be my helpers in the work of God?" The disciples said, "We will be God's helpers." (3:52)

They stand still, and if Allāh willed, He could have taken away their faculty of hearing and seeing. Certainly Allāh hath power over all things. (2:20)

They think to deceive Allāh and those who believe. (2:9)

Those who convey the message of Allāh and fear Him, and fear none save Allāh. And sufficient is Allāh as a Reckoner. (33:39)

All the praises and thanks be to Allāh, the Lord of the *'ālamīn* (mankind, *jinn*, and all that exists). (1:2)

Eat and drink of that which Allāh has provided. (2:60)

The Greatest Name

The Name of the Essence of God Bound by the Qualities of Unity and Oneness

The name Allāh is the name of the Creator and Sustainer of all the worlds and the heavens. No plural can be derived from it and it has, according to the best authorities, no root and no derivation. The word connotes all attributes of perfection and beauty in their infinitude and denotes none but the One and Unique God, the Supreme, Perfect, and Most Gracious.

The title Allāh is the essential name of God. All other titles are considered as attributes of the Divine Being. Then the attributes are called the excellent names. The Holy Qur'an says, "All the most beautiful names belong to Allah, so call on Him by them." (7:180)

This is the Majestic, Supreme name that is singular to Him, the Truth, most exalted is He. He gave this name to Himself alone, and made it His First Name, and made it completely for Him. This is the name that leads to His essence, glory be to Him; and so we are obligated to unify Him, and worship Him exclusively, and to turn to Him in times of ease and in times of hardship.

There is only one name. This is the real name, the greatest name with the essence of all the secrets. For that reason, you can say *Allāh ir-Raḥmān, Allāh al-Laṭīf*, etc. He has ninety-nine qualities, but only one name, a very special name. All the qualities begin and end in Allāh. When you look inside any quality, you will find Him. This is He. In the divine breath from the name Allāh are all the qualities, and knowledge of the meaning of the qualities leads to Him, the Supreme name, Allāh. This is distinguished from everything and also from His attribute *Al-Ilāh* which means there is no god, but the God and He is One God.

الله الله الله

Ar-Raḥmān

The Gracious
Exalted and Glorious

In the name of Allāh the Most Gracious, the Most Merciful. (1:1)

The Most Gracious, the Most Merciful. (1:3), (2:163)

They disbelieve in the Most Gracious. (13:30)

Invoke Allāh or invoke the Most Gracious, by whatever name you invoke Him, it is the same, for to Him belong the best names. (17:110)

Verily! I seek refuge with the Most Gracious from you. (19:18)

I have vowed a fast unto the Most Gracious, so I shall not speak to any human being this day. (19:26)

Oh my father! Worship not Satan: Verily Satan has been a rebel against the Most Gracious. (19:44)

Oh my father! Verily I fear lest a torment from the Most Gracious should overtake you, so that you become a companion of Satan. (19:45)

Whenever the verses of the Most Gracious were recited unto them, they fell down prostrate and weeping. (19:58)

Then indeed We shall drag out from every sect all those who were worst in obstinate rebellion against the Most Gracious. (19:69)

The connotation of this name is wide enough to cover the qualities of love, compassion, benevolence and generosity. It means the Being overflowing with the quality of mercy and always ready to pour it out upon His creation. Allāh is the Gracious because He gives blessings and prosperity to all beings without any disparity.

Allāh bestows good, blessing and happiness on all the creatures with no dispersion.

He who mentions this name one hundred times after the dawn prayer, Allāh will bestow on him a good memory, a keen conscience, and relieve him of a heavy grief.

Ar-Raḥmān means the One with Much Mercy. It is a name which is particular to Allāh and no one else can be given this name. This is because His mercy encompasses all things, and He is the Most Merciful of the merciful. So let us make mercy our banner, so that we may be immersed in the mercy of Allāh which encompasses everything.

الله الله الله

أَلرَّحِيمُ

Ar-Raḥīm

The Merciful

Exalted and Glorious

He is the One Who accepts repentance, the Most Merciful. (2:54)

Truly, You are the One Who accepts repentance, the Most Merciful. (2:128)

I am the One Who accepts repentance, the Most Merciful. (2:160)

Verily, Allāh is the One Who forgives and accepts repentance, the Most Merciful. (9:118)

Tell My slaves that truly I am the Oft-Forgiving, the Most Merciful. (15:49)

Verily Allāh is the Oft-Forgiving, the Most Merciful. (42:5)

Allāh forgives all sins. Truly He is Oft-Forgiving, Most Merciful. (39:53)

This is a revelation sent down by the All-Mighty, the Most Merciful. (36:5)

Truly, Allāh is full of kindness, the Most Merciful toward mankind. (2:143)

All the praises and thanks be to Allāh, the Lord of the ᶜā*lamīn* (mankind, *jinn*, and all that exists). The Most Gracious, the Most Merciful. (1:2-3)

Mercy may imply pity, long suffering patience, and forgiveness, all of which the sinner needs and Allāh, the Most Merciful bestows in abundant measure. But there is mercy that comes before the need arises, the grace which is ever watchful and flows from Allāh, the Most Gracious to all His creatures, protecting them, preserving them, guiding them, and leading them to clearer light and a higher life.

Allāh's mercy is in all things and for all things. All nature subserves a common purpose, which is for the good of all His creatures. Our faculties and understanding are instances of His grace and mercy. Each among His creatures benefits from the others and receives them as Allāh's mercy to itself. And in its turn, each contributes to the benefit of others and is thus an instance of Allāh's mercy to them. His mercy is universal and all pervasive.

Allāh bestows the good and blessings to those who use the gifts with which He ordered them, as Allāh bestows forgiveness on the believers on the Day of Resurrection. He who mentions this name a hundred times every day after the dawn prayer and before the morning arrives will find intimacy, as well as helpfulness, and will be tolerant toward all people living around him. Those with sincere compassion in their hearts, who recite *Ya Rahman Ya Rahim* 100 times after each obligatory prayer may be saved from forgetfulness, headlessness, and hard-heartedness. Those who recite *Ya Rahim* 100 times after each morning prayer may receive mercy and compassion from all creatures.

Ar-Raḥīm is the constant overflowing of the mercy to His believing faithful slaves. So let us be as Allāh describes, "Severe with the unbeliever, and giving mercy to each other," and let us be patient in order to receive this mercy.

الله الله الله

Al-Malik

The Sovereign
Exalted and Glorious

He could not take his brother by the law of the king, except that Allāh willed it. (12:76)

There was a king behind them who seized every ship by force. (18:79)

Then high above all be Allāh, the True King. (20:114)

Exalted be Allah, the True King. The Lord of the Supreme Throne! (23:116)

He is Allāh beside Whom none has the right to be worshiped but He, the King, the Holy, the One free from all defects, the Giver of security, the Watcher over His creatures, the All-Mighty, the Compeller, the Supreme. (59:23)

Whatsoever is in the heavens and whatsoever is on the earth glorifies Allah, the King of everything, the Holy, the All-Mighty, the All-Wise. (62:1)

The King of Mankind. (114:2)

Then high above all be Allāh, the True King. (20:114)

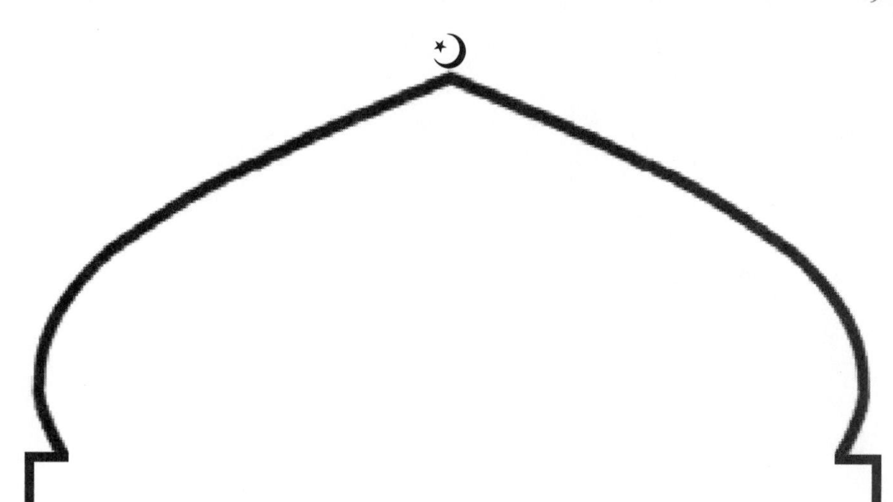

A king is he who has power and domination over people. The Supreme King is Allāh, the Exalted and the Glorious. He reigns with no one after Him.

The Sovereign is the king and the Ruler of all creations. Allāh is the Sole Sovereign of the whole human race. He is the Maker and the Master of all created things. Allāh is the True Ruler of this world and the hereafter. Allāh is the One and Only Real King Who will remain forever, and Who rules not merely over the bodies of all beings, but even over their hearts and spirits.

He who repeats this name, Allāh will bestow on him respect by others. According to tradition, Al-Kẖiḍr taught the following prayer to be recited 100 times over a sick person: *Allāhumma antal-Malik-ul-Haqq ulladhi la ilaha illa anta Ya Allāhu, Ya Salamu, Ya Shafi, Ya Shifa al-qulub.* (3 times) Our Lord, You are the True King, other than Whom there is no other god. O Allāh, O Source of Peace, O Healer, O Medicine of Hearts! If Allāh so wills, a cure will follow.

He is Allāh, King of kings, and the Kingdom belongs to Him. He is the King of the Day of Judgment; He is the King of His creation; He is the Absolute King. Let us fill our hearts with all of His Majesty. Our obedience to Him is the way to have nearness to Him, and to have Him pleased with us.

الله الله الله

أَلْقُدُّوسُ

Al-Quddūs

The Holy
Exalted and Glorious

He is Allāh beside Whom none has the right to be worshiped but He, the King, the Holy, the One free from all defects, the Giver of security, the Watcher over His creatures, the All-Mighty, the Compeller, the Supreme. (59:23)

Whatsoever is in the heavens and whatsoever is on the earth glorifies Allāh, the King of everything, the Holy, the All-Mighty, the All-Wise. (62:1)

This name is another attribute of Allāh which conveys the meaning, the sense of purity, and the freedom from all sorts of drawbacks, faults, flaws, defects, and blemishes. Allāh is the Perfect, Holy, Supreme Being Who will remain forever. Allāh is the Perfect, the Holy because He is above all human weakness.

If one with a pure heart recites *Ya Quddūs* 100 times a day, his heart will become free of all the thoughts and concerns by which we cause ourselves trouble, worry, and pain.

Al-Quddus is the Apparent – free from every defect and shortcoming, and is beyond thought forms or the grasp of the mind. So exalt Him beyond shortcomings or defects, and make your belief be in Him as He says, "There is nothing like unto Him."

الله الله الله

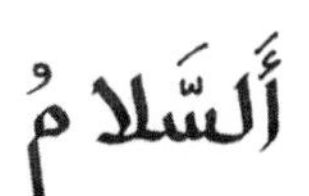

As-Salām

The Source of Peace and Safety
Exalted and Glorious

When those who believe in Our *āyāt* (signs, lessons, proofs, revelations, etc.) come to you, say, "*As-salāmun ᶜalaikum*. Peace be on you." (6:54)

They will call out to the dwellers of paradise, "*As-salāmun ᶜalaikum*. Peace be on you." (7:46)

And peace (*salām*) will be their greetings therein! (10:10)

They said: "Peace!" He answered, "Peace!" and hastened to entertain them with a roasted calf. (11:69)

Peace be upon you (*as-salāmun ᶜalaikum*) for you persevered in patience! (13:24)

Their greeting therein will be, "Peace!" (14:23)

It was said, "O Noah! Come down from the ship with peace from Us and blessings on you and on the people who are with you." (11:48)

It will be said to them, "Enter therein, in peace and security." (15:46)

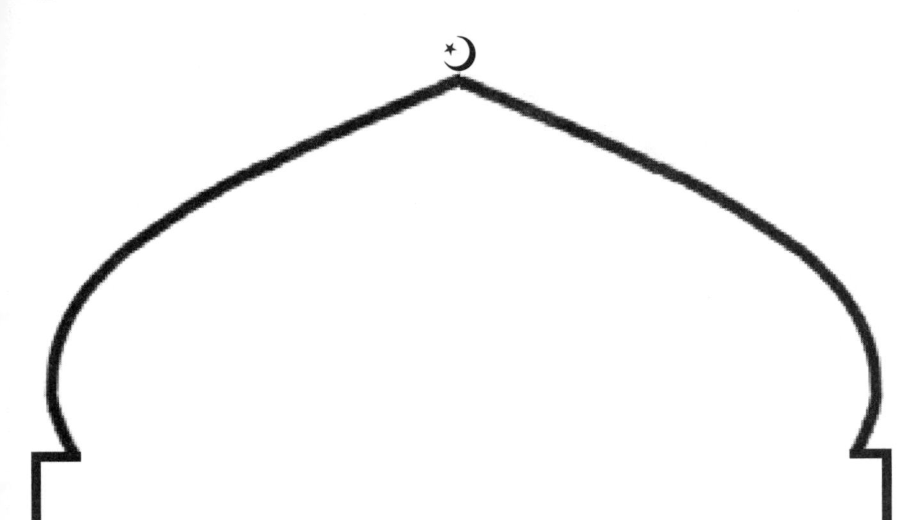

Enter you therein in peace and security – this is a Day of eternal life. (50:34)

When you go in the cause of Allāh, verify the truth and say not to anyone who greets you by embracing Islam, “You are not a believer.” (4:94)

Wherewith God guides all those who seek His good pleasure to ways of peace. (5:16)

And peace be upon me the day I was born, and the day I die, and the day I shall be raised alive! (19:33)

He is Allāh beside Whom none has the right to be worshiped but He, the King, the Holy, the One free from all defects, the Giver of security, the Watcher over His creatures, the All-Mighty, the Compeller, the Supreme. (59:23)

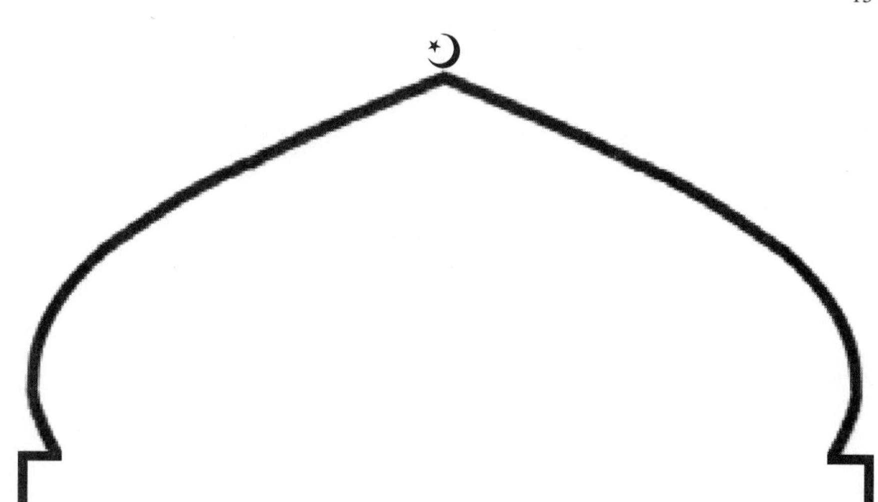

This name recognizes that all obedient servants are protected and endowed with security by Him. It is extolled that all individuals of the Muslim nations, on hearing or uttering the name of the Holy Prophet Muhammad, must send peace and blessings of Allāh upon him. He is the Peace. He who repeats this name a hundred times to a sick person will help him regain his health. *As-Salām,* the Flawless is the quality of the one who has cleaned his heart of hatred, envy, treachery, vengeance, jealousy, etc. If such a person, who is the master of his ego and under the protection of his Lord recites Ya Salām over a sick person 160 times, by the will of Allāh that person may find healing.

The name Peace is also described in the invocation:

"Allāhumma anta salām wa minka salām wa ilaika ya'oud salām fa ena bi salām yal dẖal jalali wal ikram.

"Oh Allāh, You are the Peace and from You is the peace. Give us the peace to live in this peace. No one can live without Your peace. Oh Lord of Majesty and Glory."

As-Salām is the Spreader of Peace among humanity, and He is the One whose essence is free from all defects or annihilation. Only ask from Him, and exalt Him above or beyond defects.

الله الله الله

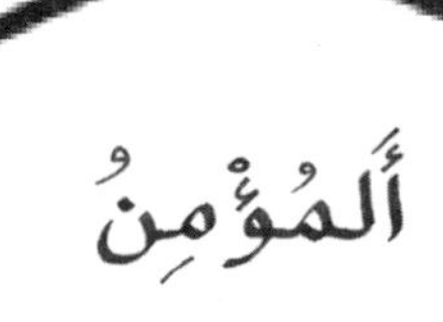

Al-Mu'min

The Bestower of Faith
Exalted and Glorious

But Allāh has endeared the faith to you and beautified it in your hearts. (49:7)

He is Allāh beside Whom there is no god but Him, the Sovereign (*al Malik*), the Holy (*al-Quddūs*), the peace (*as-Salām*), the bestower of Faith (*al-Mu'min*), the Protector (*al-Muhaymīn*), the Invincible (*al-ᶜAzīz*), the Omnipotent (*al-Jabbār*), the Most Great (*al-Mutakabbir*). (59:23)

For such He has written faith in their hearts and has strengthened them with *ruḥ* (the Spirit) from Himself. (58:22)

How should I fear those whom you associate in worship with Allāh, though they can neither benefit nor harm, while you fear not that you have joined in worship with Allāh things for which He has not sent down to you any authority. So which of the two parties has more right to be in security? If you but know. Those who have come to belief and have not obscured their faith with injustice – security is theirs and they are rightly guided. (6:81-82)

Allāh is the Bestower of Faith and the Giver of Peace. If a person in whom the name *al-Mu'min* is manifest calls on *Ya Mu'min* seventy times after *al-isha* prayer, he will be secure from harm. *Al-Mu'min* is the One Who safeguards His friends from punishment, and the One who fulfills His promise to His worshippers. So move toward His obedience so that you may be among His friends whom Allāh describes as those who are not overtaken by fear nor do they sorrow.

الله الله الله

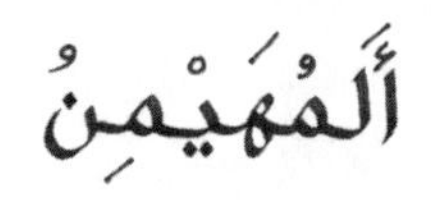

Al-Muhaymīn

The Protector
Exalted and Glorious

We have sent down to you the Book in truth, confirming the Scripture that came before it, and *Muhaymin* guarding over it. (5:48)

He is Allāh beside Whom none has the right to be worshiped but He, the King, the Holy, the One free from all defects, the Giver of security, the Watcher over His creatures, the All-Mighty, the Compeller, the Supreme. (59:23)

This name is another attribute, containing divine secrets, of Allāh, the Exalted and the Glorious, and of the Holy Qur'an. Allāh is the Protector of everything and is the Guardian of His bondsmen and a Protector of them. The Holy Qur'an is also the protector of other Holy Books. What agrees with the Qur'an in the other Holy Books is true and what disagrees is changed and untrue.

The inner being of those who recite this name with full attentiveness is luminous. If someone who is aware and attentive in his inner and outer life writes this name on a piece of silk, holds it over burning musk, amber, and sugar, recites *Ya Muhaymin* over it 5000 times a day for seven days, then puts it under his pillow, by the will of Allāh, he will dream of the events which will affect his material and spiritual life in the future.

Al-Muhaymīn watches and protects everything. He is the Overseer of the actions of His creation, the Decider of provision and life-span, the One Who ensures welfare and well-being. So worship Him as He deserves to be worshiped; if you do not see Him, know that He sees you.

الله الله الله

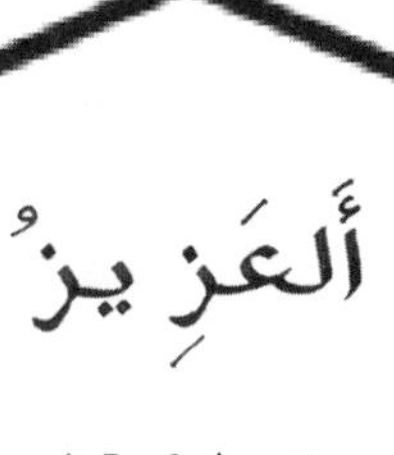

Al-ᶜAzīz

The Exalted in Might

Then know that Allāh is All-Mighty, All-Wise. (2:209)

Truly Allāh is All-Mighty, All-Wise. (2:220)

But men have a degree of responsibility over them. And Allāh is All-Mighty, All-Wise. (2:228)

And Allāh is All-Mighty, All-Able of Retribution. (3:4)

Verily, Allāh is All-Mighty, All-Wise. (8:10)

Certainly, Allāh is All-Mighty, All-Able of Retribution. (14:47)

Verily! You are the All-Mighty, All-Wise. (2:129)

Such is the measuring of the All-Mighty, the All-Knowing. (6:96)

Verily, your Lord – He is the All-Strong, the All-Mighty. (11:66)

For Allāh is the highest description. And He is the All-Mighty, All-Wise. (16:60)

Verily, your Lord will decide between them by His Judgment. And He is the All-Mighty, the All-Knowing. (27:78)

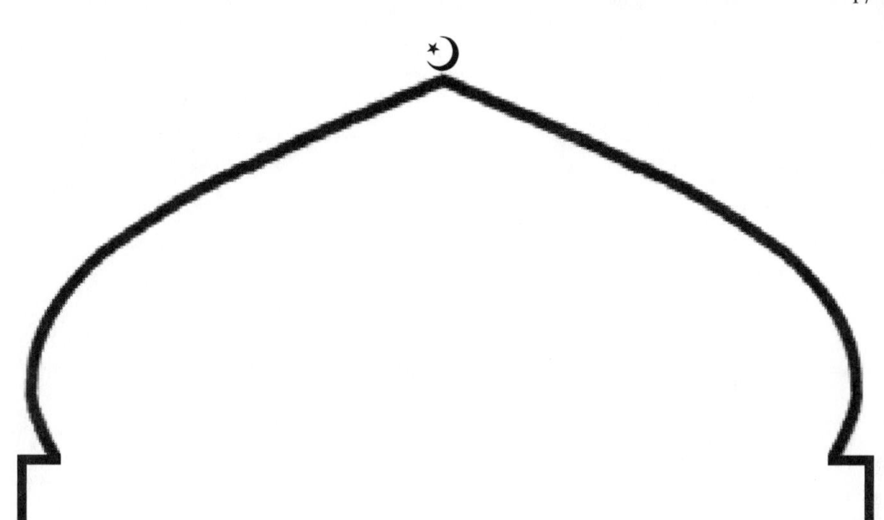

This name is derived from the word which means dignity, majesty, and power. Allāh holds command over the heavens and the earth and whatsoever is between them. His hand is over all His works.

One who repeats this name forty times after the morning prayer for forty days will not only become self-sufficient but will be independent of need from others.

Al-ᶜAzīz alone has strength. Outwardly He is not overtaken by any strength. He has power over everything. If you desire strength in both worlds, obey the *ᶜAzīz* as He says, "Strength is for Allāh, and the messenger, and for the believers."

الله الله الله

Al-Jabbār

The Irresistible
Exalted and Glorious

He is Allāh beside Whom there is no god but Him, the Sovereign (al Malik), the Holy (*al-Quddūs*), the peace (*as-Salām*), the bestower of Faith (*al-Mu'min*), the Protector (*al-Muhaymīn*), the Invincible (*al-'Azīz*), the Omnipotent (*al-Jabbār*), the Most Great (*al-Mutakabbir*). (59:23)

This name is derived from the word *jabbār* which means correctitude. When this word is used as an attribute of Allāh, it means the Comforter of the disheartened.

He who recites this name and sincerely believes in the power of Allāh will not be compelled to do anything against His wishes, and will not be exposed to violence, severity, or hardness. Hadrat 'Ali used to pray, "*Ya Jabbira kulli kasirin wa ya musahilla kulli 'asirin*. O Jabbār, Who puts together all that is broken and brings ease to every difficulty–"

Al-Jabbār is the One Whose will over-rides everything. No one is outside the influence of His power. He has power over His creation in what He wills, so surrender to His decree, and know that nothing that strikes you could have missed you.

الله الله الله

أَلْمُتَكَبِّرُ

Al-Mutakabbir

The Majestic
Exalted and Glorious

He is Allāh beside Whom there is no god but Him, the Sovereign (*al-Malik*), the Holy (*al-Quddūs*), the peace (*as-Salām*), the bestower of Faith (*al-Muʾmin*), the Protector (*al-Muhaymīn*), the Invincible (*al-ʿAzīz*), the Omnipotent (*al-Jabbār*), the Most Great (*al-Mutakabbir*). (59:23)

This name is derived from majesty. Allāh is the True Majestic. He is above all. He shows His greatness in all things and in all ways.

He who repeats this name before having union with his beloved wife will be blessed by Allāh with a righteous child.

Al-Mutakabbir is the One exalted beyond the attributes of creation. He is unique in His greatness, so be humble to the One described by these attributes, and beware of being arrogant with people.

الله الله الله

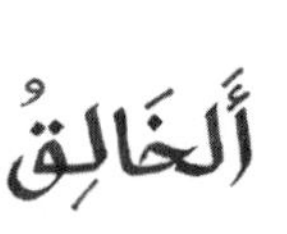

Al-Kh̲ālīq

The Creator

Exalted and Glorious

Such is Allāh, your Lord! There is no god but He, the Creator of all things. (6:102)

Say: "Allāh is the Creator of all things." (13:16)

And remember when your Lord said to the angels: "I am going to create a man from dried sounding clay." (15:28)

Remember when your Lord said to the angels: "Truly I am going to create man from clay." (38:71)

Allāh is the Creator of all things and He is the Guardian and Disposer over all things. (39:62)

That is Allāh, your Lord, the Creator of all things. There is no god but He. None has the right to be worshiped but He. How then are you turning away? (40:62)

He is Allāh, the Creator, the Inventor of all things, the Bestower of Forms. (59:24)

So Blessed is Allāh, the Best of creators. (23:14)

Verily your Lord is the All-Knowing Creator. (15:86)

Is not He Who created the heavens and the earth, able to create the like of them? Yes, indeed! He is the All-Knowing, Supreme Creator. (36:81)

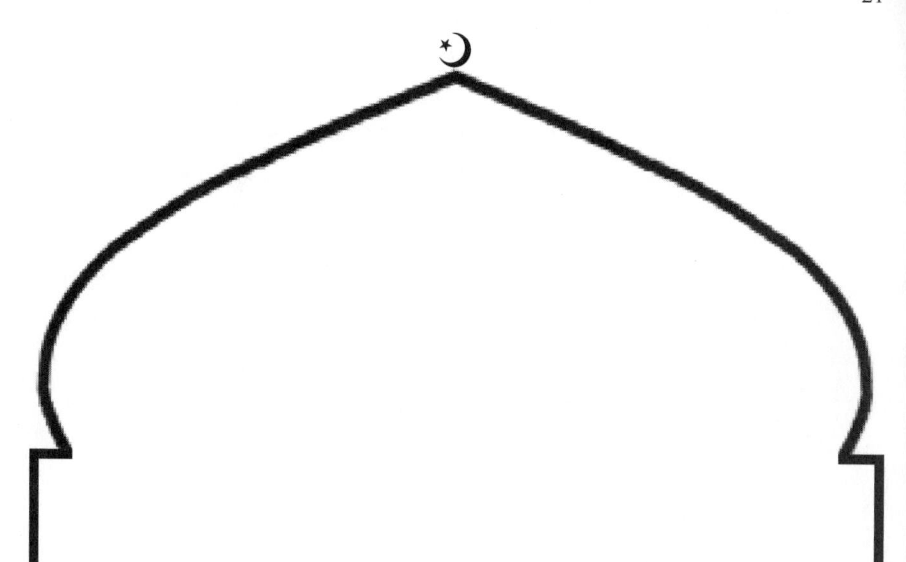

This name is an attribute of Allāh meaning that it is Allāh Who is the only One Who has created the heavens and the earth, Allāh Who is the only One Who has created night, Allāh Who is the only One Who has created life and death.

To the one who repeats this name at night, Allāh will appoint an angel for his security and protection until the Day of Judgment. The reward for this angel's action will be given to that person.

Al-Kẖāliq is the Originator of everything. The One Who has power over everything. The One Who gives existence to things from nothingness. He is the Creator of every craftsman, and His crafts reflect upon the creation of Allāh, and then praise Him for the greatness of His crafts.

الله الله الله

Al-Bāri᾽

The Maker
Exalted and Glorious

So turn in repentance to your Maker. (2:54)

Truly I am innocent of what you join in worship with Him. (6:19)

Verily, I have turned my face toward Him Who has created the heavens and the earth, and I am not of those who give partners to Allāh. (6:79)

The name the Maker is the Evolver. Allāh has created all things in proportion. He is the Molder of each form and frame. He is the Designer Builder of earth and of heaven.

This name is used to induce labor for a woman whose time to give birth has arrived, but she is having difficulty. She fasts for seven days and each day, at the time of breaking fast, she repeats three names of Allāh: the Creator, the Maker, and the Fashioner, twenty-one times each. She then breathes into a cup of water and drinks this water. Allāh will bless her with a child.

Al-Bāri᾽ is the One Who created the creation with His power, not by making a copy of something previous. He is the One with the power to manifest what He wills into existence. My believing brother, the One Who creates surely is deserving of being worshiped; so be sincere in your worship of Allāh.

الله الله الله

أَلْمُصَوِّرُ

Al-Muṣawwir

The Fashioner

Exalted and Glorious

> He is Allāh, the Creator, the Inventor of all things, the Bestower of forms. To Him belong the best names. All that is in the heavens and on earth glorify Him. And He is the All-Mighty, the All-Wise. (59:24)

This name gives definite form or color, so as to focus a thing directly towards a goal.

If a woman has been unable to bear a child and she keeps fast for seven days, and recites *Ya Kẖāliq*, *Ya Bāriʾ*, *Ya Muṣawwir*, and breaks her fast every evening with a drink of water over which the sacred name of Allāh has been recited twenty-one times, she will be blessed with a child.

Al-Muṣawwir is the One who gives everything its form. He fashions it in a way that each has its own unique form which distinguishes it from any other; so do not look down upon anyone, because the One Who fashioned you and fashioned him is Allāh.

الله الله الله

Al-Gẖaffār

The Great Forgiver
Exalted and Glorious

And verily, I am indeed forgiving to him who repents, believes and does righteous good deeds, and then remains constant in doing them. (20:82)

The Lord of the heavens and earth and all between, Exalted in Might, able to enforce His will forgiving again and again. (36:66)

Is not He the Mighty (*al-ᶜAziz*), He Who forgives (*al-Gẖaffār*) again and again? (39:5)

And I invite you to the All-Mighty, the Oft-Forgiving! (40:42)

And I have said seek pardon of your Lord. Lo! He is ever Forgiving (*al-Gẖaffār*). (71:10)

People commit sins, but Allāh with His infinite Mercy forgives faults. He who recites this name 33 times, Allāh will forgive his sins.

Al-Gẖaffār is the only One Who forgives all wrong-doing, and veils defects in this world and the next; so increase your asking for forgiveness, rush into repentance, and do not despair of the Mercy of Allāh.

The Messenger of Allāh says, “Whoever forgives and hides the wrongdoing of another, Allāh will forgive him and hide his sins on the Day of Judgment.” If a person has compassion in his heart toward the things he sees around him and recites *Ya Gẖaffār* 100 times after *jummah* prayers, Allāh may forgive his faults of the previous week. When anger flares up in your heart, if you remember and recite *Ya Gẖaffār*, it may subside.

الله الله الله

أَلْقَهَّارُ

Al-Qahhār

The Irresistible Subduer
Exalted and Glorious

Are many Lords differing among themselves better, or Allāh the One, Supreme and Irresistible. (12:39)

Say: "Allāh is the Creator of all things, and He is the One, the Supreme, the Irresistible." (13:16)

They will appear before Allāh, the One, the Irresistible. (14:48)

Say (to the people), "I am only a warner, and there is no god except Allāh, the One, the Irresistible." (38:65)

This name is derived from a word meaning dominance. The Dominant is One Who has greater commanding influence even on the influential. The human being can claim that he holds complete dominance over another human being, but Allāh has full control over our body, spirit, and movement. He is Dominant in a way in which He can do anything He wills. The qualities of *al-Qahhar* and *al-Latif* are within each other.

Repeat this name sixty-six times to control worldly desires, and gain spiritual contentment and inner peace. The repetition of this name also protects you from doing evil deeds.

Al-Qahhār, the Vanquisher Who overcomes His creation by His authority and power. He is the One who drives them into what He wills, voluntarily or involuntarily. Everything submits to His majesty, so submit to the Order of Allāh, and to His prohibitions, and do not disobey Him.

الله الله الله

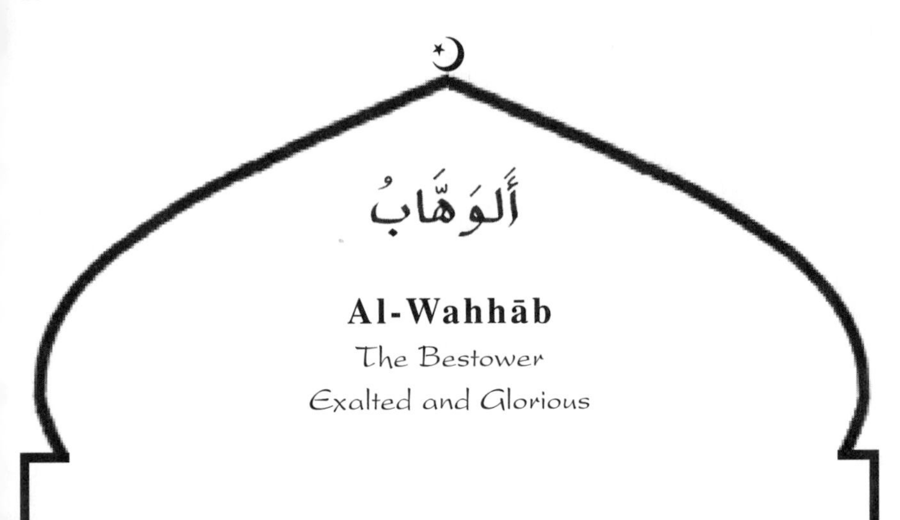

Al-Wahhāb

The Bestower
Exalted and Glorious

Our Lord! Let not our heart deviate from the truth after You have guided us, and grant us mercy from You. Truly, You are the Bestower. (3:8)

My Lord! Forgive me, and bestow upon me a kingdom such as shall not belong to any other after me. Verily, You are the Bestower. (38:35)

This is the Great and Permanent Bestower. The Prophet Ibrahim, may Allāh be pleased with him, was turned out of the borders of his country by the king, but Allāh bestowed upon him enormous wealth. He gave him two sons, ᵓIsmaᶜil and ᵓIsḥāq, may Allāh be pleased with them. ᵓIbrāhīm thanked Allāh for the blessing of their birth. Allāh is the Bestower because He is the real Owner of all sorts of gifts, whether visible or invisible, worldly or in the hereafter. This name tells us that man owns nothing. Whatever he owns he holds only with the Munificence of Allāh.

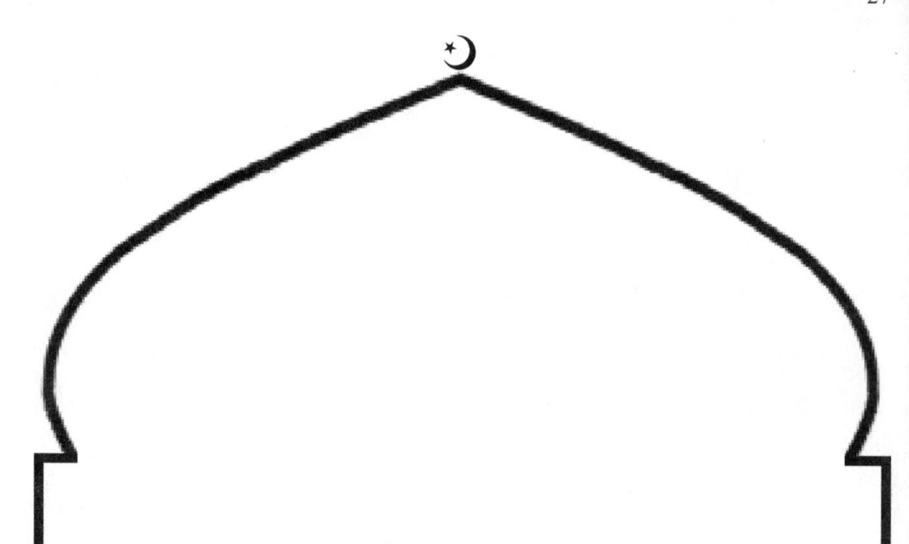

He who repeats this name seven times after the morning prayer, appealing to Allāh, his prayer will be answered. A needy person, or one who has been captured by an enemy, or someone who cannot earn enough money to suffice himself, if he repeats this name three to seven nights, one hundred times after the two bows of optional prayer at midnight, Allāh will bless him with all his needs and free him from the clutches of an enemy.

Al-Wahhāb is the Bestower to His slaves, the One Who bestows without wage, the One Who gives without being asked, the Giver of many gifts, and He continuously gives. So do not ask anyone but Him, and do not rely on anyone but Him, and thank Him for His giving.

الله الله الله

Ar-Razzāq

The Provider

Exalted and Glorious

Verily, Allāh is the All-Provider. (51:58)

This name is an attribute of Allāh. All actions that lead to support are under the direction of the Real King, the Lord and Creator of all creation, and at His will and pleasure. As a sign of our gratitude for His beneficence and blessings showered on us, we must feed the hungry and help the needy.

He who recites this name will be provided with sustenance by Allāh. Those who hang this name in their work place may become more successful. Recite *Ya Razzāq* 100 times after *jummah* prayer for stress and depression.

Ar-Razzāq is the One Who offers provision and gives all of His creatures their provision. He is the Provider of everything that needs anything; the Preserver of life. There is no other provider, and do not expect your provision from other than Him, and do not abase yourself to other than Him.

الله الله الله

Al-Fattāh

The Opener
Exalted and Glorious

> Our Lord! Reveal (open) the truth between us and our people, and You are the Best of Revealers. (7:89)

> He will decide between us by the truth. And He is the Opener (of the truth), the All-Knower of the true state of affairs. (34:26)

This attribute of Allāh has two meanings – opening and success. On the Day of Resurrection truth will be opened. It is Allāh alone Who opens the door of success in overcoming all the troubles and obstacles encountered by us, Who opens our hearts to the truth, Who makes knowledge flow from our tongues, Who unveils the accomplishments of different sciences before our eyes, and Who makes the believers profess.

We appeal to Allāh with this invocation: "Oh Allāh! I ask you to endow me with Your blessings of all kinds, from the beginning to the end, complete in all respects, in this worldly life as well as the life of the hereafter, and grant me salvation and high rank among the denizens of paradise." He who repeats this name sixty times, Allāh will enlighten his mind and he will be given victory.

He is the Opener of closed matter and the Easer of difficulty. He holds in His hands the keys to the heavens and the earth. Be in expectancy of receiving His generosity. Be in vigil of release, and be content with His decree.

الله الله الله

أَلعَلِيمُ

Al-^{c}Alīm

The All-Knowing
Exalted and Glorious

And He is the All-Knower of everything. (2:29)

Allāh is All-Hearer, All-Knower. (3:34)

Whatever of good you spend, Allāh knows it well. (3:92)

And whatever good they do, nothing will be rejected of them; for Allāh knows well those who are the pious. (3:115)

Thus does Allāh make clear to you (His Law) lest you go astray. And Allāh is the All-Knower of everything. (4:176)

We raise whom We will in degrees. Certainly your Lord is All-Wise, All-Knowing. (6:83)

The chiefs of the people of Pharaoh said, "This is indeed a well-versed sorcerer." (7:109)

Others are made to wait for Allāh's Decree, whether He will punish them or will forgive them. And Allāh is All-Knowing, All-Wise. (9:106)

Verily, He is the All-Knower of the innermost secrets of the breasts. (11:5)

They said, "Do not be afraid! We give you glad tidings of a son possessing much knowledge and wisdom." (15:53)

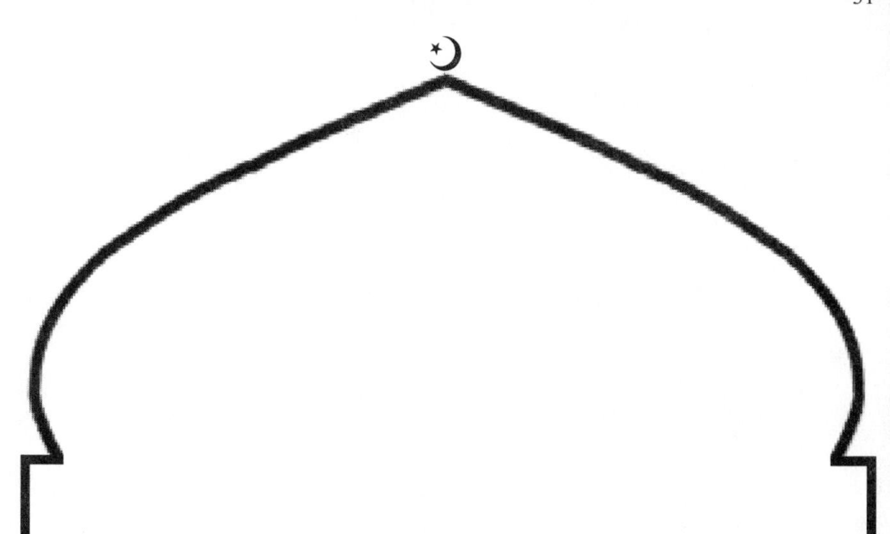

In the verses of the Holy Qurʾān in which this name, which is an attribute of Allāh, is mentioned, His knowledge is manifested completely in all respects and encompasses the knowledge of everything that exists. He knows the secrets in the heart of man, and He knows what he utters with his tongue. He alone knew what was secret and what was hidden in the case of Pharaoh and the sorcerers.

He who recites this name one hundred times, his heart will be luminous, revealing the divine light.

Al-ᶜAlīm is the One Who knows the details of affairs, and the intricacies of things, and the hidden things of the hearts and the souls. Nothing is hidden from His knowledge, not even an atom's worth. His knowledge encompasses everything, so do not be deluded by His beautiful veiling, and be ashamed of yourself before Him in the open and in secret.

الله الله الله

As-Samīᶜ

The All-Hearing
Exalted and Glorious

So Allāh will suffice for you against them.
And He is the All-Hearer, the All-Knower. (2:137)

Whoever changes the bequest after hearing it,
the sin shall be on those who make the change.
Truly, Allāh is All-Hearer, All-Knower. (2:181)

And make not Allāh's name an excuse in your oaths against doing good and acting piously, and making peace among mankind. And Allāh is All-Hearer, All-Knower. (2:224)

Offspring, one of the other, and Allāh is All-Hearer,
All-Knower. (3:34)

At that time Zakariya invoked His Lord, saying, "Oh my Lord! Grant me from You, a good offspring. You are indeed the All-Hearer of invocation." (3:38)

And if an evil whisper comes to you from Satan, then seek refuge with Allāh. Verily, He is All-Hearer, All-Knower. (7:200)

He, Muhammad, (may the peace and blessings of Allāh be upon him), said, "My Lord knows every word spoken in the heavens and on earth. And He is the All-Hearer, the All-Knower." (21:4)

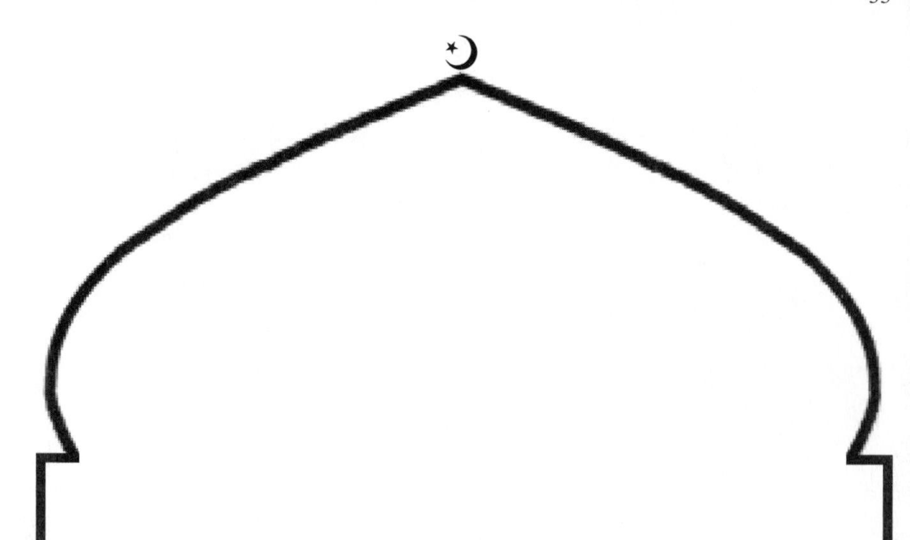

This attribute of Allāh means that Allāh hears all sounds whether soft or loud. He is the One and the only Being who will remain forever. He listens to all the prayers and sounds of creatures without disruption.

Allāh loves His bondsman who is ever praying, pleading and begging Him for favors.

He who recites this name one hundred times without speaking to anyone on Thursdays after *al-asr* until *maghrib* prayer, Allāh will bestow any desire on him.

Nothing is hidden from Him on earth or in the heavens. Nothing is beyond His hearing. Even if it is hidden He encircles all that can be heard, so call upon Him in times of ease and in times of difficulty.

الله الله الله

Al-Baṣīr

The All-Seeing One
Exalted and Glorious

And Allāh is All-Seer of what they do. (2:96)

And Allāh will be pleased with them. And Allāh is All-Seer of His slaves. (3:15)

And fight them until there is no more disbelief (*fitnah*) and the religion will all be for Allāh alone. But if they cease (worshipping others besides Allāh), then certainly, Allāh is All-Seer of what they do. (8:39)

Therefore stand firm and straight as you are commanded, and those (your companions) who turn unto Allāh in repentance with you, and transgress not (from the path). Verily, He is All-Seer of what you do. (11:112)

Glorified and Exalted is He above all that they associate with Him Who took His slave Muhammad, may His peace and blessings be upon him, for a journey by night from *al-Masjid-al-Ḥarām* at Mecca to *al-Masjid-al-ᶜAqsa* in Jerusalem, the neighborhood whereof We have blessed, in order that We might show him, Muhammad, may His peace and blessings be upon him, of Our *ayat* (signs). Verily, He is the All-Hearer, the All-Seer. (17:1)

That is because Allāh merges the night into the day, and He merges the day into the night. And verily, Allāh is All-Hearer, All-Seer. (22:61)

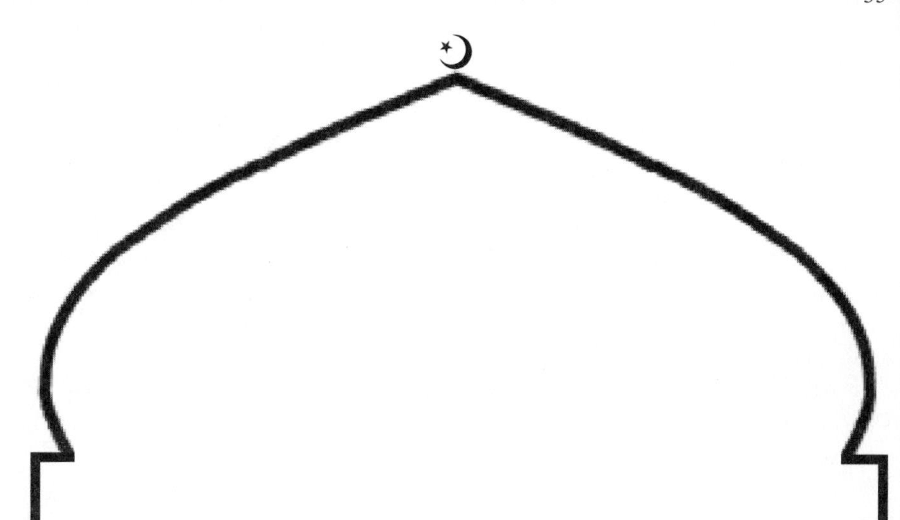

The creation of you all and the resurrection of you all are only as the creation and the resurrection of a single person. Verily, Allāh is All-Hearer, All-Seer. (31:28)

This is one of the attributes of Allāh which carries the meaning of the ability to see. He sees all things. Even the steps of a black ant on a black stone on a dark night. We should supplicate Allāh with purity of thought and implicit faith.

He who repeats this name one hundred times between the first four bows of the tradition of the Holy Prophet and the obligatory prayer at the Friday prayer, Allāh will give this person esteem in the eyes of others.

Al-Baṣīr is the One Who Sees everything in its outward and its inward. He encircles everything that is visible. So worship Allāh as if you see Him. And if you do not see Him, know that He sees you.

الله الله الله

أَللَّطِيفُ

Al-Laṭīf

The Subtle One

Exalted and Glorious

> No vision can grasp Him, but He grasps all vision. He is *Al-Latif*, the Most Subtle and Courteous, Well-Acquainted with all things. (6:103)
>
> Certainly, my Lord is the Most Courteous and Kind unto whom He wills. (12:100)
>
> Verily Allāh is Subtle (understands the finest mysteries), Well-Aware of its place. (31:16)
>
> And He is the Most Kind and Courteous to His slaves, All-Aware of everything. (67:14)

It is not easy to define in words what this attribute of Allāh implies. It may imply fine subtlety, so fine and subtle as to be imperceptible to human sight, so pure as to be incomprehensible with sight, so perfect as to see and understand the finest subtleties and mysteries, so kind and extraordinarily gracious as to bestow gifts of the most refined kind. He who has become poor and helpless, if he repeats this name one hundred times after the two bows of the optional prayer, his desires will be fulfilled.

Al-Laṭīf is the One Who is gentle with His creatures. He gives them provision. He makes them easy. He is generous towards them and showers them with His gifts. So be gentle with the slaves of Allāh and be soft with them, and be gentle when you call them.

الله الله الله

Al-Kẖabīr

The Aware

Exalted and Glorious

When they have fulfilled their term, there is no sin on you if they (the wives) dispose of themselves in a just and honorable manner. Allāh is well-acquainted with what you do. (2:234)

There did Allāh give you one distress after another by way of requital to teach you not to grieve for that which had escaped you, nor for that which had befallen you. And Allāh is Well-Aware of all that you do. (3:153)

He is the Irresistible, above His slaves; and He is the All-Wise, Well-Acquainted with all things. (6:18)

His will be the dominion the day when the trumpet will be blown. All-Knower of the unseen and the seen. He is the All-Wise, Well-Aware of all things. (6:73)

And remember that which is recited in your houses of the verses of Allāh and His Wisdom. Verily Allāh is Ever Most Courteous, Well-Acquainted with all things. (33:34)

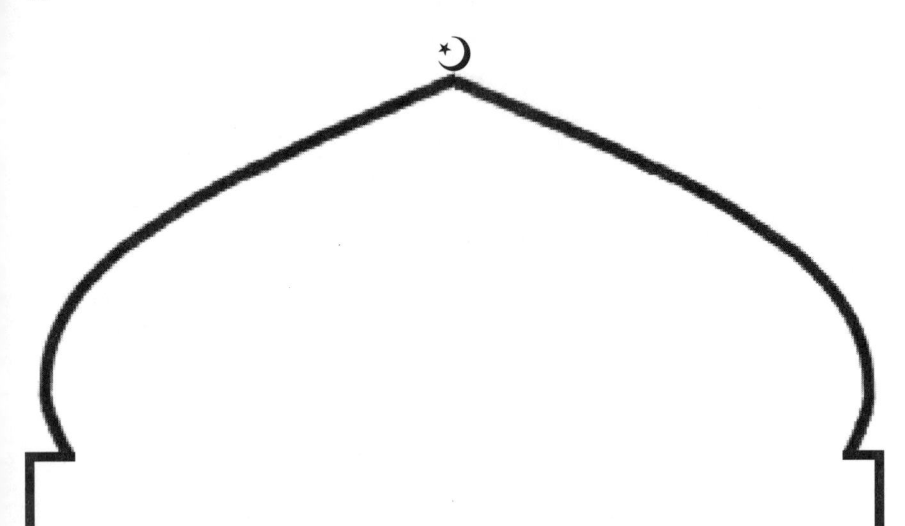

This name, *Al-Khabīr*, is an attribute of Allāh, for He is the Omniscient Who knows, witnesses and sees all things and is aware of all conditions anywhere.

He who has a bad habit and wants to get rid of it, if he repeats this name continuously (as often as he can), he will be quickly freed from this habit by the grace of Allāh.

Al-Khabīr is the One Who has knowledge of the details of matters. Nothing is hidden from Him, and nothing is absent from His knowledge. He has knowledge of everything that has been, and everything that will be. So be careful with everything that you say and do.

الله الله الله

أَلْحَلِيمُ

Al-Ḥalīm

The Clement

Exalted and Glorious

Allāh will not call you to account for that which is unintentional in your oaths, but He will call you to account for that which your hearts have earned. And Allāh is Oft-Forgiving, Most-Forbearing. (2:225)

The seven heavens and the earth and all that is therein, glorify Him and there is not a thing but glorifies His Praise. But you understand not their glorification. Truly He is Ever-Forbearing, Oft-Forgiving. (17:44)

This name means tolerance, forbearance, serenity, affability, and wisdom. Allāh's mercy overcomes His anger and He is ever inclined to forgive on penitence.

When one writes this name on a piece of paper and puts it in the place where seed is sown, no harm or calamity will befall the crop, if Allāh so wishes. When one is angry, if he recites this name, *Ya Ḥalīm* 88 times, his anger may subside. To help restore affection in a marriage, write this name on an apple, and eat it.

Al-Ḥalīm is the Patient One Who gives time but does not ignore. He veils sins and He delays punishments. He provides for the sinful in the same way as He provides for the obedient; so take on this quality in your life, and have patience and excuse people, and be in the most excellent way with them.

الله الله الله

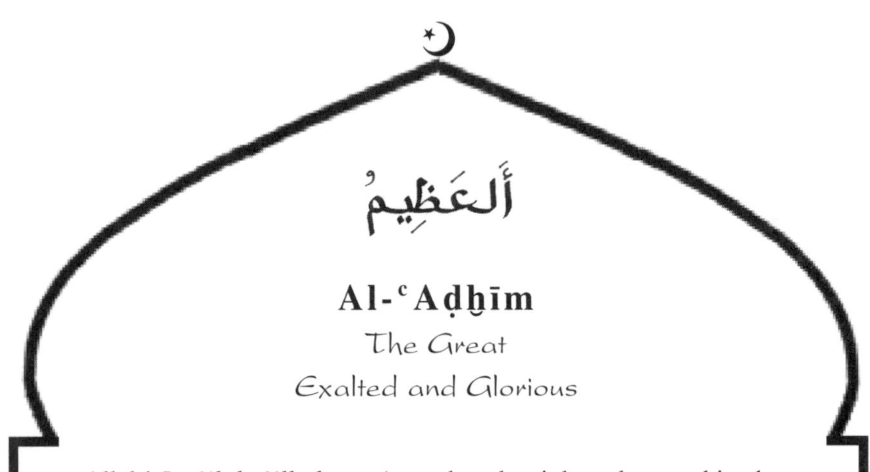

Al-ᶜAḏẖīm

The Great

Exalted and Glorious

Allāh! *Lā ᵓilāhaᵓilla ḥuwa* (none has the right to be worshiped but He), the Ever-Living. Neither slumber nor sleep overtaketh Him. To Him belongs whatever is in the heavens and whatever is on the earth. Who is he that can intercede with Him except with His permission? He knows what happens to them in this world, and what will happen to them in the Hereafter. And they will never encompass anything of His Knowledge except that which He wills. His *Kursi* extends over the heavens and the earth, and He feels no fatigue in guarding and preserving them. And He is the Most High, the Most Great. (*Ayat-ul-Kursi* 2:255)

This name is above everything in divinity and He is the One and the Only Being Who will remain forever. There is no god save Him, the Ever-Living, the Eternal. He is the Creator of the great heavens, the Most Bounteous, the Greatest of all. His Foot-stool spreads over the heavens and the earth. He is the Savior of all beings from all trials and tribulations. He gives honor and power to whom He likes. He has bestowed the Holy Qur'an on His servants for their guidance and salvation. He who repeats this name many times will be respected by others.

The Prophet, may the blessings and peace of Allāh be upon him, said, "He who learns, teaches what he knows, and acts upon his knowledge is called 'Abdul 'Azhim in heaven."

Al-ᶜAḏẖīm is the One Whose greatness has no beginning, and His Majesty has no end. Nothing is like unto Him, so be in awe of His Majesty, and be satisfied with what He allots to you.

الله الله الله

أَلْغَفُورُ

Al-Ghafūr

The All-Forgiving
Exalted and Glorious

Truly Allāh is Oft-Forgiving, Most Merciful. (2:173)

They thought there would be no *fitnah* (punishment), so they became blind and deaf. After that Allāh turned to them (with forgiveness), yet again many of them became blind and deaf. And Allāh is the All-Seer of what they do. (5:71)

But your Lord is Most Forgiving, full of Mercy. (18:58)

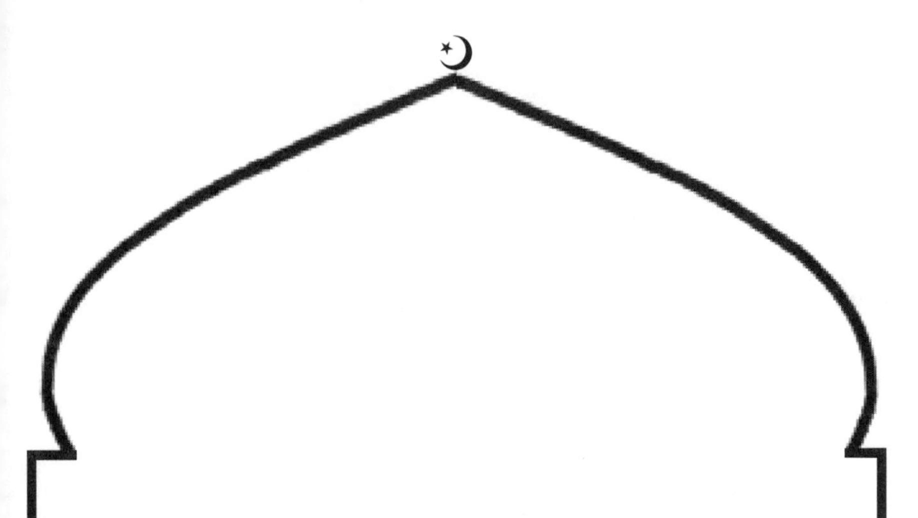

This name denotes forgiving of sins. There is salvation from Allāh for His servants as He is the All-Forgiving. He accepts gratitude and is affectionate towards all.

Allāh is Oft-Forgiving, Most Merciful. When we suffer from trials and tribulations, it is for our good and no one can remove them except Allāh.

He who has a headache or is suffering from a fever, if he repeats this name continuously, will be relieved of his ailment. If someone feels guilty and is therefore heavy of heart, reciting *Ya Gẖafūr* 100 times after *jummah* prayer on Friday may relieve the pain; and if Allāh wishes, He will forgive that sin.

Al-Gẖafūr is the One who puts a veil on the wrongdoing of His slaves and their sins. Constantly ask for His forgiveness and turn to Him in repentance.

الله الله الله

Asẖ-Sẖakūr

The Appreciative
Exalted and Glorious

Why should Allāh punish you if you have thanked Him and believed in Him. And Allāh is Ever All-Appreciative, All-Knowing. (4:147)

That He may pay them their wages in full, and give them more out of His Grace. Verily He is Oft-Forgiving, Most Ready to appreciate. (35:30)

And they will say, All the praise and thanks be to Allāh Who has removed from us all grief. Verily, Our Lord is indeed Oft-Forgiving, Most Ready to appreciate. (35:34)

Verily, We showed him the way, whether he be grateful or ungrateful. (76:3)

Allāh is the Appreciative because He recognizes good actions and rewards us beyond all measure. *Asẖ-Sẖakūr* is more than *ash-Shakir*.

He who has a heavy heart and repeats this name forty-one times over a glass of water, then washes his face with this water, his heart will lighten, and he will be able to maintain himself. The Messenger of Allāh, may the blessings and peace of Allāh be upon him, said, "He who is not thankful to people will not be able to be thankful to Allāh."

Asẖ-Sẖakūr is the One Who increases the few actions of His slaves. He rewards them in multiples. His thanks to His slaves is to forgive them; so increase your thanks and praise Him and exalt Him.

الله الله الله

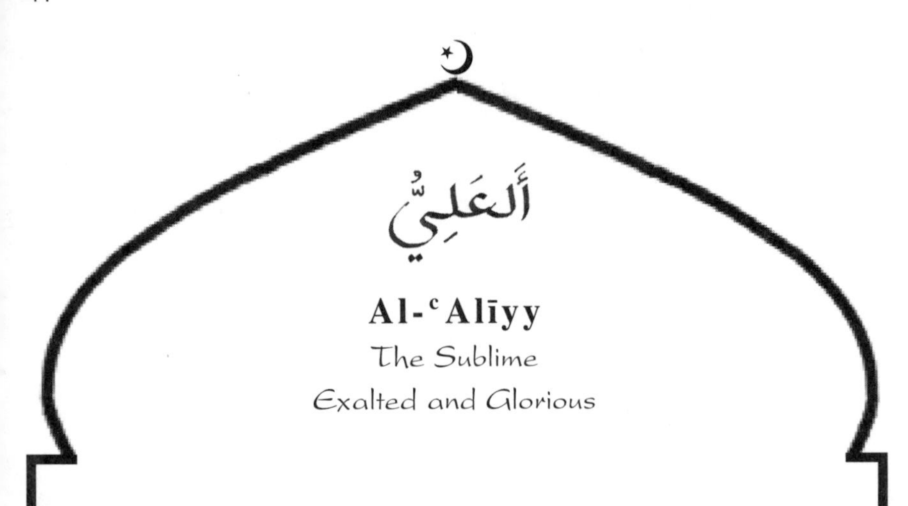

Al-^{c}Alīyy

The Sublime

Exalted and Glorious

His Throne doth extend over the Heavens and the earth and He feeleth no fatigue in guarding and preserving them, for He is the Most High, the Supreme (in Glory). (2:255)

We said: “Fear Not! For Thou indeed hast the upper Hand.” (20:68)

They are but vain falsehood: Verily God is He, Most High, Most Great. (22:62)

They will say that which is true and just; and He is the Most High, Most Great. (34:23)

But such as come to Him as Believers who have worked righteous deeds, for them are ranks exalted. (20:75)

Saying: “I am your Lord, Most High.” (79:24)

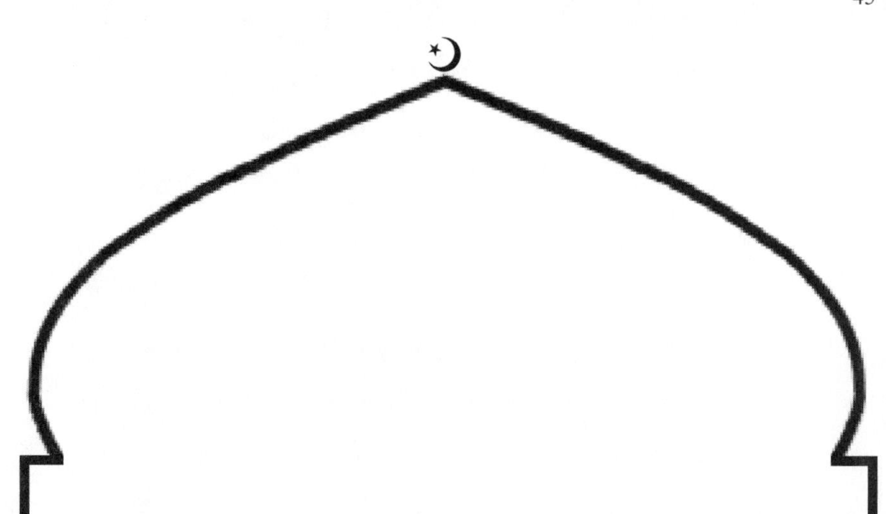

This attribute of Allāh means eminence, greatness, supremacy, grandeur and loftiness. Allāh is Sublime and Omnipotent. He is Superior and above everything in Divinity.

He whose faith is weak and he repeats this name thirty-three times, his faith will become sound and correct, and he will reach his destination. This name benefits whoever carries it written upon his person and recites it as often as possible.

Al-ᶜAlīyy is the One of High Rank Whose description does not do Him justice. He is beyond competitors or opposers. All exalted meanings are established in Him. So be humble and be meek between the Hands of your Creator.

الله الله الله

ألكبير

Al-Kabīr

The Most Great
Exalted and Glorious

The Knower of the unseen and the seen, the Most Great, the Most High. (13:9)

And what they invoke besides Him, it is falsehood. And verily, Allāh – He is the Most High, the Most Great. (22:62)

That is because Allāh, He is the Truth, and that which they invoke besides Him is falsehood, and that Allāh, He is the Most High, the Most Great. (31:30)

Intercession with Him profits not except for him whom He permits. So much so that when fear is banished from their hearts, they say, "What is it that your Lord has said?" They say, "The Truth. And He is the Most High, the Most Great." (34:23)

Al-Kabīr is the Great, the Exalted in His attributes and actions. He has no need for anything, and nothing is beyond His reach. Nothing is like Him, so remember the greatness of your Lord in all times by honoring His commands and His prohibitions.

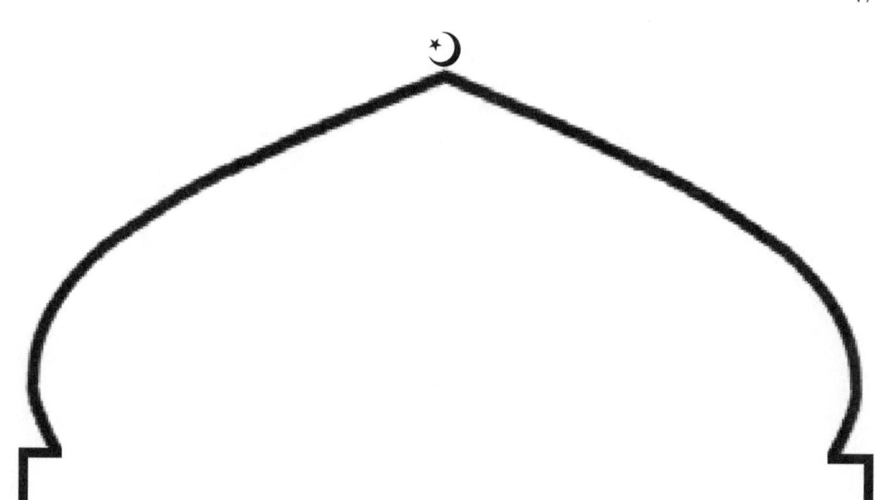

This name means greatness, pride and dignity. He is the Creator and Sustainer of all the creation, of all the worlds, of the heavens and the earth, and of all the places between the heavens and the earth which were shown to the Holy Prophet Muhammad, may the peace and blessings of Allāh be upon him. Allāh is pure and free of all evils, vices, and defects.

He who repeats this name one hundred times daily will become honorable and respectable in the eyes of people. If one has lost his job or has a debt he cannot pay, if he fasts for 7 days and each night upon breaking the fast recites, "*Ya Kabiru anta iladhi la tahdil-'uqulu li wasfi 'azamatihi;* O Greatest, You are the One Whose Magnificence intellects are unable to describe," 1000 times, if Allāh wants he will receive a position and be able to pay his debt. To recite *Ya Kabīr* 232 times over some food and feed it to a couple who are having marital troubles, may help solve their problems.

الله الله الله

أَلْحَفِيظُ

Al-Ḥafiḍẖ

The Preserver
Exalted and Glorious

Verily proofs have come to you from your Lord, so whosoever sees will do so for the good of his own self, and whosoever blinds himself will do so to his own harm, and I (Muhammad, may Allāh's peace and blessings be upon him) am not a watcher over you. (6:104)

So if you turn away, still I have conveyed the message with which I was sent to you. My Lord will make another people succeed you, and you will not harm Him in the least. Surely my Lord is Guardian over all things. (11:57)

That which is left by Allāh for you is better for you, if you are believers. And I am not a guardian over you. (11:86)

And he (Iblis) had no authority over them – except that We might test him who believes in the Hereafter from him who is in doubt about it. And your Lord is *Ḥafiḍẖ*, Watchful over everything. (34:21)

And as for those who take protectors other than Him, Allāh is *Ḥafiḍẖ*, Watcher over them, and you, (Oh Muhammad, may Allāh's peace and blessings be upon him) are not a *Wakil* over them. (A guardian or a disposer of their affairs.) (42:6)

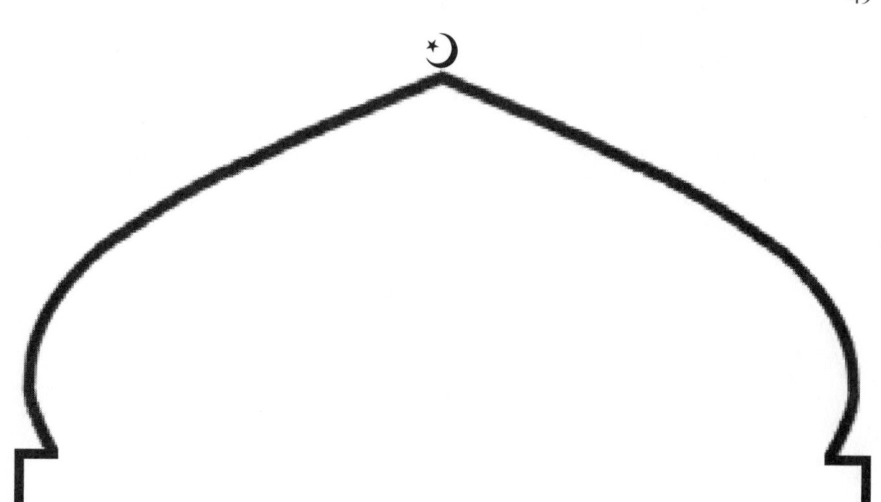

This name is an attribute of Allāh plainly describing the meaning of guarding, watching, protecting, custody and preserving. He is *Ḥafiḍẖ* meaning the Lord Preserver of all the worlds. Only Allāh assigns the angels for protecting us from evils, defeats the evil designs of Satan against us, safeguards the chastity of His obedient womenfolk, and bestows on us the Holy Book, which contains guidance for us.

He who repeats this name sixteen times each day, Allāh will protect him from calamities.

Al-Ḥafiḍẖ is the One Who protects everything even though it be the size of an atom. He does not disregard anything. There is not an atom's worth of anything lost from the gaze of His protection. He does not change, and He is not annihilated. Change does not occur to Him from the outside. Nothing from the outside influences Him. He protects His creation. So remember Allāh in times of ease and in times of difficulty, and He will protect you with His protection.

الله الله الله

Al-Muqīt

The Maintainer

Exalted and Glorious

> Whosoever intercedes for a good cause will have the reward thereof, and whosoever intercedes for an evil cause will have a share in its burden. And Allāh is Ever All-Able to do everything. (4:85)

This name is an attribute of Allāh which means the Guardian. Allāh is the Sustainer, the Maintainer of all creation.

If anyone has a bad-mannered child and he repeats this name thirty-three times over a glass of water and gives the water to the child to drink, the child will have good manners.

Al-Muqīt is the One Who is the Provider. He is the One Who gives sustenance to all His creation. He is the *Ḥafiḍẖ*. He is the One Who has power over everything, and the Fashioner of destinies, and the One Who gives all kinds of spiritual sustenance. So seek the good (*halal*) in your provision, since He is the guarantor of it.

الله الله الله

أَلحَسِيبُ

Al-Ḥasīb

The Reckoner
Exalted and Glorious

Whoever (of the guardians of orphans) is rich, he should take no wages, but if he is poor let him have for himself what is just and reasonable. And when you release their property to them, take witness in their presence; and Allāh is All-Sufficient in taking account. (4:6)

When you are greeted with a greeting, greet in return with what is better than it, or at least return it equally. Certainly, Allāh is Ever a Careful Account Taker of all things. (4:86)

(It will be said to him): "Read your book. You yourself are sufficient as a reckoner against you this Day." (17:14)

Those who convey the Message of Allāh and fear Him, and fear none save Allāh. And Sufficient is Allāh as a Reckoner. (33:39)

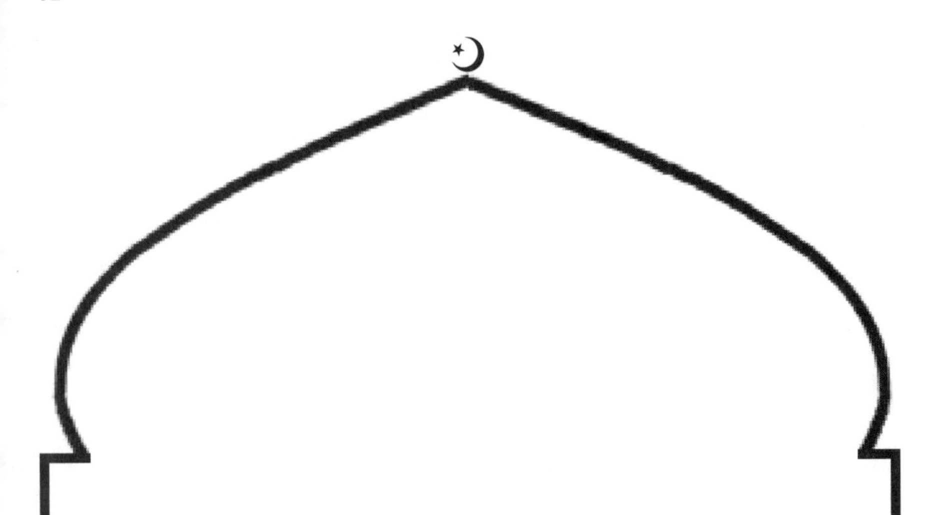

This name is an attribute of Allāh meaning the Reckoner on the Day of Judgment. All our deeds are recorded and we will be rewarded or punished accordingly.

If one is afraid of being robbed, or is afraid of the jealousy of an envious one, or is afraid of being harmed or wronged, he may begin on a Thursday to repeat this name seventy times a day and night for seven days, and at the seventy-first time, if he says, "Allāh is my Reckoner," he will be free of his fears, if Allāh, the Most High wills.

If one writes this name on a bottle and feeds a colicky baby from it, his crying may stop.

Al-Ḥasīb is the Sufficient (*al-Kāfīy*) Who suffices His creation. He is the One Whom we rely upon. He is the One Who is sufficient for His creation by His overflowing generosity, and Who takes care of troubles. So be certain in your certainty of Allāh that Allāh is sufficient for you and is very complete for you. Turn your face to Allāh and put your reliance upon Him.

الله الله الله

أَلْكَرِيمُ

Al-Karīm

The Generous

Exalted and Glorious

So Exalted be Allāh The True King. *Lā ᵓilaha ᵓilla ḥuwa*, none has the right to be worshiped but He, the Lord of the Supreme Throne. (23:116)

Truly his gratitude is for the good of his own self, and whoever is ungrateful, he is ungrateful only for the loss of his own self. Certainly my Lord is Rich, Free of all needs, Bountiful. (27:40)

Oh man! What has made you careless about your Lord, the Most Generous. (82:6)

This name is the Most Bountiful attribute of Allāh because He sustains all creatures and provides them with food and with all the necessities of life. The mercy of Allāh is always found by those who sincerely repent and show it by their conduct. One who recites this name seventy-seven times will have esteem in this world and in the hereafter.

Al-Karīm is the Generous. He is the One Who is overflowing with goodness, the Giver Who does not cease to give. He is the Generous, the Absolutely Generous, the Gatherer of all goodness, nobility, and exalted qualities. So turn to Him with all your senses in taking care of your needs.

الله الله الله

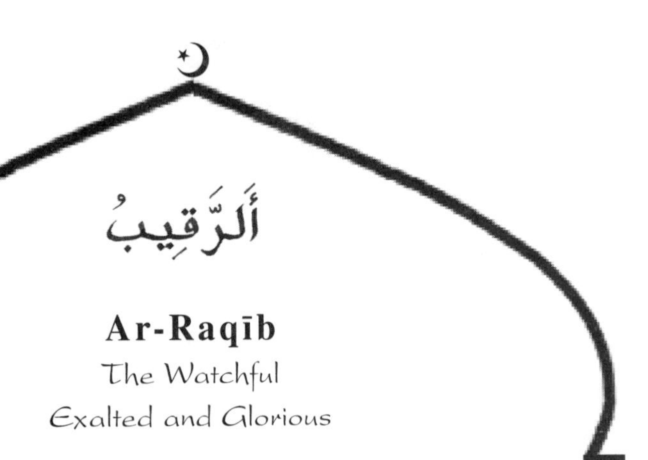

Ar-Raqīb

The Watchful

Exalted and Glorious

Oh mankind! Be dutiful to your Lord, Who created you from a single person and from him He created his wife, and from them both He created many men and women; and fear Allāh through Whom you demand your mutual rights, and do not cut the relations of the wombs. Surely, Allāh is Ever an All-Watcher over you. (4:1)

Never did I say to them aught except what You did command me to say, "Worship Allāh, my Lord and your Lord." And I was a witness over them while I dwelt among them, but when You took me up, You were the Watcher over them, and You are a Witness to all things. (5:117)

And Allāh is Ever a Watcher over all things. (33:52)

This is one of the ninety-nine attributes of the Almighty which means the Watchful. He watches all His creatures, and guards us and secures us from the evil designs of Satan.

He who repeats this name seven times over himself, his family, and his property will be under the Protection of Allāh. If a person in the station of witnessing recites this name as often as possible in a hidden place for a month, the eye of his heart will see secrets which others cannot see. He may even understand the language of beasts, vegetation, and lifeless things.

Al-Raqīb is the Watcher Who watches over the states of His slaves, for He knows what they are saying and counts their deeds. He is the Surrounder from Whom nothing is hidden; so fear Allāh, and be attentive to all your movements and your stillnesses.

الله الله الله

أَلْقَرِيبُ

Al-Qarib

The Ever-Near
Exalted and Glorious

When my slaves ask you (Oh Muhammad, may the peace and blessings of Allāh be upon him) concerning Me, then answer them, I am indeed Near to them by My Knowledge. I respond to the invocations of the supplicant when he calls on Me. (2:186)

He brought you forth from the earth and settled you therein. Then ask forgiveness of Him and turn to Him in repentance. Certainly, my Lord is Near, Responsive. (11:61)

Say: "If I go astray, I shall stray only to my own loss. But if I remain guided, it is because of the Revelation of my Lord to me. Truly, He is All-Hearer, Ever Near to all things." (34:50)

The meaning of this name of the ninety-nine names of Allāh is that He is near at hand. We need no mediator between Allāh and us. He is so near to every bondsman that we can invoke Him and place our requests before Him wherever we may be. So much so that He hears and answers those requests, which are not expressed in words, but are made only in the innermost heart. He who recites this name one hundred and one times will draw nearer to Allāh.

الله الله الله

He brought you forth from the earth and settled you therein, then ask forgiveness of Him and turn to Him in repentance. Certainly, my Lord is Near, Responsive. (11:61)

This name is an attribute of Allāh which means the One Who answers prayer.

He who repeats this name fifty-five times, his appeal will be answered.

Al-Mujib is the Responsive Who receives supplications and questions which He then grants. So turn to Allāh with your supplications, for He is the Answerer to whomever calls upon Him.

الله الله الله

أَلْوَاسِعُ

Al-Wāsi[c]

The All-Embracing
Exalted and Glorious

To Allāh belongs the east and the west, so wherever you turn there is the Face of Allāh. Surely! Allāh is All-Sufficient for His creatures' needs, All-Knowing. (2:115)

He said, "Verily, Allāh has chosen him above you, and has increased him abundantly in knowledge and stature. And Allāh grants His kingdom to whom He wills. And Allāh is All-Sufficient for His creatures' needs, All-Knower." (2:247)

Say, Oh Muhammad, may the peace and blessings be upon him, "All the bounty is in the Hand of Allāh. He grants to whom He wills. And Allāh is All-Sufficient for His creatures' needs, All-Knower." (3:73)

But if they separate Allāh will provide abundance for every one of them from His Bounty. And Allāh is Ever All-Sufficient for His creatures' needs, All-Wise. (4:130)

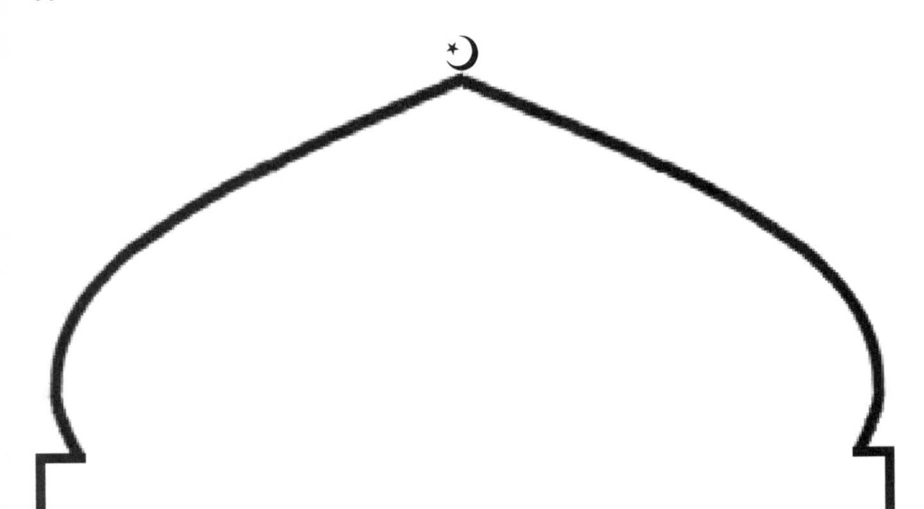

This name manifests Allāh's greatness, munificence, power and might. It clearly reveals that Allāh's generosity is beyond any limit. His bounties encompass all creatures and things, and the vastness of His knowledge is far more than the entire expanse of the earth and the heavens. ^{c}Abdul Wāsi^{c} has wisdom which is all-inclusive.

There is an invocation which refers to this name of Allāh. "Oh Allāh! We cannot see You nor think and imagine You, nor is it in our power to offer sufficient praises and gratitude for Your munificence and the bounties showered on us. We particularly solicit more of Your favors in our old age."

If he who has difficulty in earning his livelihood repeats this name, his income will be increased if God, the Most High, wills. He who is under heavy loads of work and responsibility, may find strength and relief by continually repeating this name. The sickness of envy and revenge may find a çure in the repetition of this name. Reciting Ya Wāsi^{c} 137 times when depressed may relieve the depression.

Al-Wāsi^{c} is the Expansive Who extends His Provision over the creation, and spreads His Mercy over everything, and is the Surrounder of all things. So if you know this, do not ask about the safeguarding and provision of every species.

الله الله الله

أَلْحَكِيمُ

Al-Ḥakīm

The Wise

Exalted and Glorious

And if you slide back after the clear signs have come to you, then know that Allāh is All-Mighty, All-Wise. (2:209)

And if Allāh had wished, He could have put you into difficulties. Truly, Allāh is All-Mighty, All-Wise. (2:220)

Allāh wishes to make clear what is lawful and what is unlawful to you and to show you the ways of those before you, and accept your repentance, and Allāh is All-Knowing, All-Wise. (4:26)

We raise whom We will in degrees. Certainly your Lord is All-Wise, All-Knowing. (6:83)

Thus Allāh makes clear His *ayat* for you. And Allāh is All-Knowing, All-Wise. (24:59)

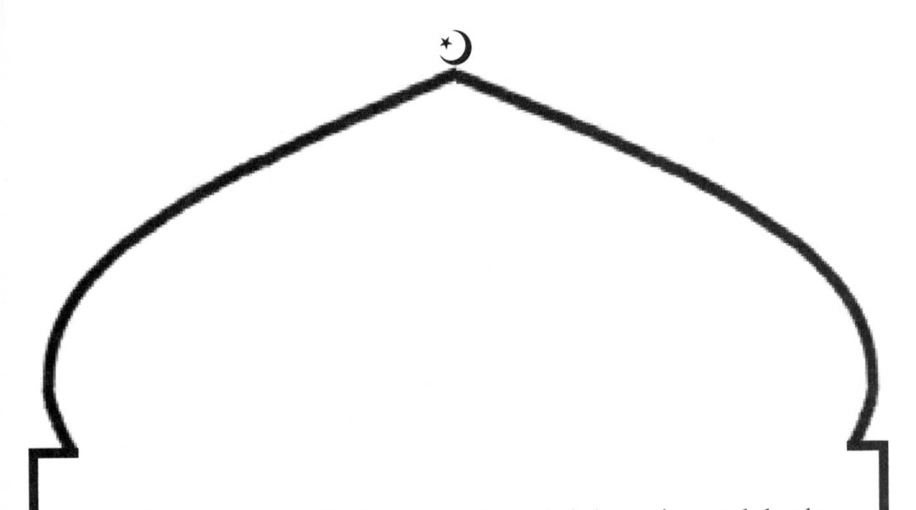

This name manifests knowledge of right action and deeds. It covers the laudable objects and purposes connected with the creation of all things, and has appeared alongside the name of the Mighty in twenty-four contexts in the Holy Qur'an.

He who recites this name from time to time will not have difficulties in his work or his tasks.

Al-Ḥakīm is the One Who is All-Wise, the Confirmer in the disposing of all subtlety, and the Appraiser of goodness in the realities of His orders. He is All-Knowing of the wisdom of what He has fore-ordained. He gathers together the decree for the creation for its goodness, its judgment and justice. He determines everything in His decrees. So know that everything has its wisdom and instruction.

الله الله الله

أَلوَدُود

Al-Wadūd

The Loving

Exalted and Glorious

Ask forgiveness of your Lord, then turn unto Him in repentance. Verily, my Lord is Most Merciful, Most Loving. (11:90)

And He is Oft-forgiving, full of love. (85:14)

This name is another attribute of Allāh, the One Who is loved, adored and worshiped. His obedient servants love Him and He loves them.

If there is a dispute between two people, and one of them repeats this name one-thousand times over some food and gives it to the other to eat, the disagreement will end. Hadrat Ali said, "If you wish to be loved by your Lord, draw close to those who abandon you. Give to those who are stingy toward you. Forgive those who harm you.

Al-Wadūd is considered by some as the greatest name. "My servant draws not near Me with anything more loved by Me than the religious duties I have enjoined upon him and My servant continues to draw near to Me with superogatory works so that I shall love him. When I love him, I am his hearing with which he hears, his seeing with which he sees, his hand with which he strikes, and his foot with which he walks." (*ḥadīth*)

Prophet Muhammad, may Allāh's blessings and peace be upon him, said, "If a believer looks at the face of another believer with love, it is better for him than praying in my mosque for a whole year."

Al-Wadūd is the Loving One, the Beloved of all His slaves, and the Beloved in the hearts of His friends. So love those whom Allāh loves of the creation, and love what Allāh loves of their deeds.

الله الله الله

They said, "Do you wonder at the Decree of Allāh? The Mercy of Allāh and His Blessings be upon you, O the family of Ibrahim. Surely, Allāh is All-Praiseworthy, All-Glorious." (11:73)

Owner of the Throne of Absolute Authority, the Glorious. (85:15)

This name of the ninety-nine names of Allāh clearly reveals honor, rank, dignity, glory, nobility, eminence and excellence. It is also used as an affix with the Holy Qur'an. He who repeats this name will live in this world honorably.

If a believer of good character who has psoriasis fasts during the 13th, 14th, and 15th of the lunar months and at fastbreak recites *Ya Majīd* 100 times, this has been know to be of help and to also assist in cases of heart disease and depression.

Al-Majīd is the Generous One. The clear victory in the end is in Him, the Manifold in excellence, the Abundant Giver, the Mighty Creator. So praise be to Allāh for His favor, for He is the most Generous One to His slaves.

الله الله الله

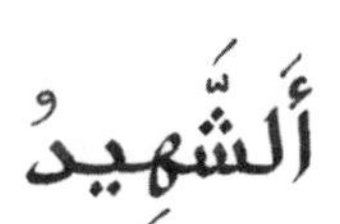

Asẖ-Sẖahīd

The Witness

Exalted and Glorious

Say: "Oh people of the Scripture! Why do you reject the *ayat* of Allāh, while Allāh is Witness to what you do?" (3:98)

Whatever of good reaches you is from Allāh, but whatever of evil befalls you, it is from yourself. And We have sent you (Muhammad, may peace and blessings be upon him) as a messenger to mankind and Allāh is Sufficient as a Witness. (4:79)

Say: "What thing is the most great in witness?" Say: "Allāh, the Most Great is Witness between me and you." (6:19)

This name clarifies that Allāh witnesses Himself as the only One to be worshiped with no partner. Allāh is All-Powerful and All-Wise. He is called the Witness because He is Omnipresent, sees and knows everything, and every single thing is under His control and knowledge. He is also called so because He is present everywhere and observes all things.

A person guilty of wrong-doing may be able to control his actions if he recites *Ya Sẖahīd* in a series of 21 repetitions at a time. This same recitation is made while pointing the index finger on the head of a rebellious and disobedient child to make the child more obedient.

Asẖ-Sẖahīd is the Witness, the Ever-Present from Whom nothing is hidden. He is the Seer of everything, and the Witness Who is the All-Knowing of every explanation. So fear Allāh Who sees you, and Who witnesses you always.

الله الله الله

Al-Ḥaqq

The Truth

Exalted and Glorious

Then High above all be Allāh, the True King. And be not in haste (Oh Muhammad, Allāh's peace be on him) with the *Qur'ān* before its revelation is completed to you, and say, "My Lord increase me in knowledge." (20:114)

That is because Allāh, He is the Truth, and it is He Who gives life to the dead, and it is He Who is able to do all things. (22:6)

And that those who have been given knowledge may know that it (this *Qur'ān*) is the truth from your Lord. (22:54)

That is because Allāh, He is the Truth, and what they invoke besides Him, it is falsehood. And verily, Allāh, He is the Most High, the Most Great. (22:62)

Allāh is the Truth. This name is repeated in the Holy *Qur'ān* two-hundred twenty-seven times. No doubt the *Qur'ān* is truth in its entirety.

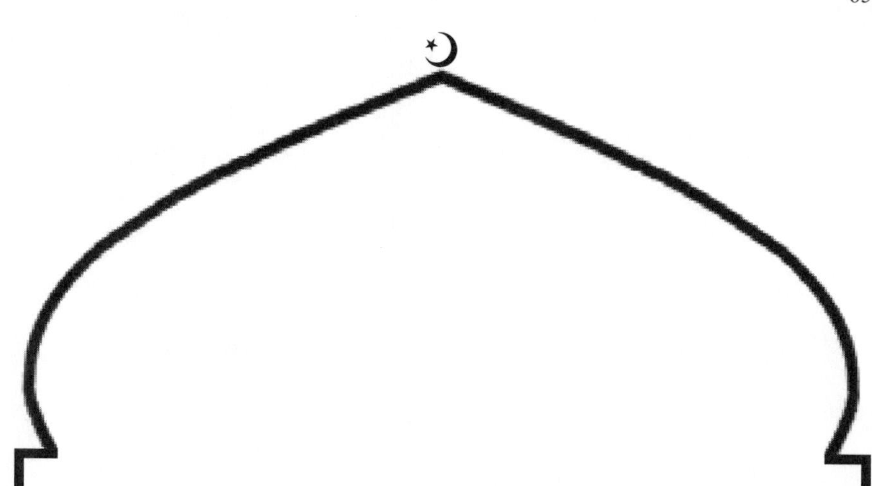

The literary meanings of truth are many and varied, the most important being to speak and act upon the unchanged truth. The Day of Judgment is sure to come, and on that Day the virtuous and evil deeds of all people will be judged. Allāh has truly created the Heavens and the Earth. The Holy Qur'an has been revealed with truth and it will lead us on the right path. Allāh is He Who reveals the Truth, nullifies falsehood, calls people to His religion of surrender to Him, gives glad tidings of the Hereafter, and administers justice with the Truth.

Worship and prayer are justified only to the One True God. Reciting, "*Lā ilāha'illa-llāh ul-Malik ul-Ḥaqq ul-Mubin*. There is no god but Allāh, the King, the Clear Truth," 100 times each day, may lead one to receive his sustenance from unexpected places. If one has lost something and repeats this name, he will find what is lost.

Al-Ḥaqq is the Truth Who establishes the truth by His words, and He is the Helper of His friends, for He is the Vindicator of His slaves. Therefore He obliges you to confirm His words in your holding fast to His Book and to the example of His Prophet, may His peace be upon him.

الله الله الله

Al-Wakīl

The Trustee, The Guardian
Exalted and Glorious

The people (hypocrites) said, "Verily, the people have gathered against you, therefore fear them." But it only increased them in faith and they said, "Allāh alone is the Sufficient for us and He is the Best Disposer of affairs for us (a most excellent protector)." (3:173)

So turn aside from them (do not punish them), and put your trust in Allāh. And Allāh is Ever All-Sufficient as a Disposer of affairs (*wa kafā bi-llāhi wakīlā*). (4:81)

Such is Allāh, your Lord! *Lā ilāha᾽illa-huwa*, the Creator of all things. So worship Him alone and He is the *Wakīl* over all things (everything is under His care). (6:102)

Had Allāh willed, they would not have taken others besides Him in worship. And We have not made you a watcher over them nor are you a *wakīl* (guardian) over them. (6:107)

I (Muhammad, may peace and blessings be upon him) am not set over you as a *wakīl*. (A disposer of affairs to oblige you for guidance.) (10:108)

Do you then feel secure that He will not cause a side of the land to swallow you up, or that He will not send against you a violent sand-storm? Then you shall find no *wakīl* to guard you from the torment. (17:68)

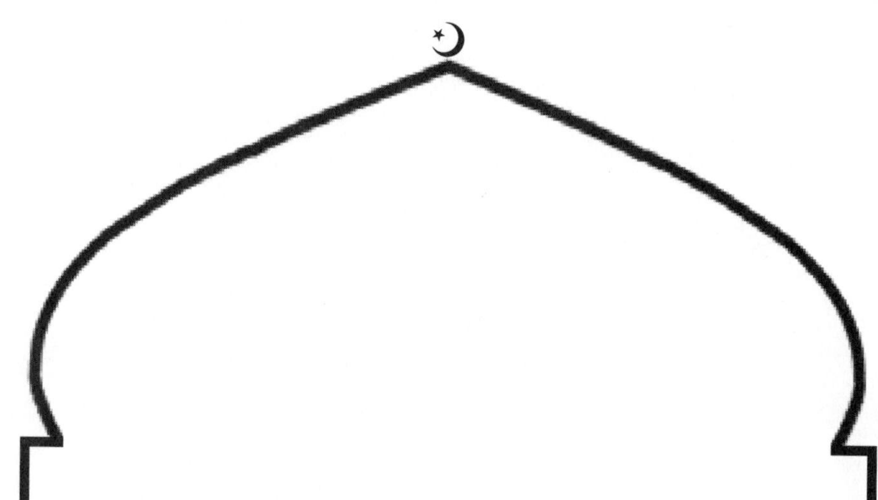

This name of Allāh manifests His full power and complete control over everything. There are blessings from Allāh and His Prophet, may Allāh's blessings and peace be upon him, for those who place their confidence in Allāh and rely on Him at all times and under all circumstances. They are rewarded and raised to high ranks in this world as well as in the Hereafter. Allāh is called the Trustee because He provides a means to solve all problems in the best way.

Those with faith in God who are afraid of drowning in water, being burnt in a fire, or any similar danger, who repeat this name in series of 66's, will be under the protection of Allāh.

Al-Wakīl is the Guardian, the Supporter of the everlasting creation through His orders. So whoever trusts in Him, He appoints sufficiency for him. So whoever is enriched and well-pleased by Him is confirmed by His help for him, and in the serenity of His safeguarding and care for him.

الله الله الله

Al-Qawiyy

The Most Strong
Exalted and Glorious

They rejected the *ayat* of Allāh, so Allāh punished them for their sins. Verily, Allāh is All-Strong, Severe in punishment. (8:52)

Verily, your Lord – He is the All-Strong, the All-Mighty. (11:66)

Verily, Allāh will help those who help His Cause. Truly Allāh is All-Strong, All-Mighty. (22:40)

They have not estimated Allāh His Rightful Estimate. Verily, Allāh is All-Strong, All-Mighty. (22:74)

This name is an attribute of Allāh which manifests His power. Allāh bestows powers on His creatures according to their capacities. Allāh protects the bondsmen from mischief, and endows their bodies and souls with all sorts of physical and spiritual powers.

One who recites this name 116 times every day, if they are weak or tired of doing their daily prayers, will find strength and enjoy them. He who cannot defeat his enemy, who repeats this name with the intention of not being harmed, his enemy will not overcome him, if Allāh, the Most High, wills.

Al-Qawiyy is the Strong, the Companion of destiny, the Imposer of complete victory, the All-Dominant Vanquisher Whose power is above all power and strength. Therefore there is no asking for might except from Him Who is the All-Mighty, nor for greatness from any but Him Who is the Giver of Destiny. For He is Allāh, the only One.

الله الله الله

أَلْمَتِينُ

Al-Matīn

The Firm

Exalted and Glorious

Surely Allah is he Who is the Provider, the Possessor of Unshakeable Might. (51:58)

This name, the Firm, is one of the names of Allāh, the Eternal and Everlasting, which clearly indicates that He is the Almighty Being Who controls the entire universe and all creation without effort. Allāh is All-Powerful, and He Alone has the power to provide food and all means of livelihood for all creatures. He who has difficulties, if he repeats this name, his troubles will disappear if Allāh, Most High, wills.

Al-Matīn is the One who is Firm. The All-Powerful Who does not dispute about anything that He wishes to realize of His wisdom, nor does He need any army or any other help to support Him in carrying out what He desires to do. So cut off any returning to anyone else but Him; for there is no other Helper for you than He.

الله الله الله

Al-Waliyy

The Protecting Friend
Exalted and Glorious

Allāh has full knowledge of your enemies, and Allāh is Sufficient as a *Waliyy*, and Allāh is Sufficient as a Helper. (4:45)

Oppressed among men, women, and children, whose cry is, "Our Lord! Rescue us from this town whose people are oppressors; and raise for us from You one who will protect, and raise for us from You one who will help." (4:75)

Say: "Shall I take as a *Waliyy* any other than Allāh, the Creator of the heavens and the earth?" (6:14)

Him whom Allāh guides, he is the rightly guided; but him whom He sends astray, for him you will find no *Waliyy* to lead him to the right path. (18:17)

This attribute of Allāh is a name which manifests love, nearness and guardianship. Allāh is the only Protecting Friend in the real sense for everyone. He who repeats this name is likely to be a friend of Allāh.

If the faithful recite this name 1000 times on Friday nights all material and spiritual barriers will disappear. In a marriage, keeping this name in mind during quarrelsome encounters may stop the fighting.

Al-Waliyy is the Protector Who is the Lover Who conceals whoever is disobedient, and He is the Helper of His friends and the Subjugator of His enemies. He is the One Who oversees and safeguards the continuation of nobility of character. So be of the friends of Allāh in your obedience and support them and increase their numbers.

الله الله الله

And know that Allāh is Rich, Free of all wants, and Worthy of all praise. (2:267)

They said, "Do you wonder at the Decree of Allāh? The Mercy of Allāh and His Blessings be on you, Oh the family of Ibrahim. Surely, He, Allāh is All-Praiseworthy, All-Glorious." (11:73)

And Moses said, "If you disbelieve, you and all on earth together, then verily Allāh is Rich, Free of all needs, Owner of all praise." (14:8)

And whoever gives thanks, he gives thanks for the good of his own self. And whoever is unthankful, then verily, Allāh is All-Rich, Free of all needs, Worthy of all praise. (31:12)

To Him belongs all that is in the heavens and all that is on the earth. And verily, Allāh – He is Rich, Free of all needs, Worthy of all praise. (22:64)

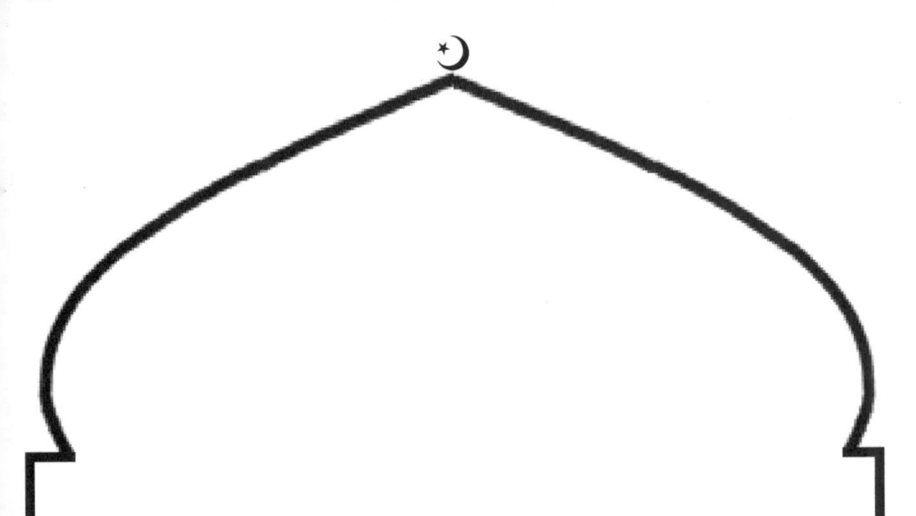

This name clearly reveals that we must praise and love Allāh, be grateful to Him, and adore and worship Him with sincerity, purity, and with our complete heart and soul. Allāh is the Creator, Controller and Sustainer of all creation, and He is the most Beneficent and Merciful. All praises, merits, and virtues originate from Him. Allāh is the only One to be praised and glorified and thanked by all creatures.

He who repeats this name will be loved and respected by the world. Reciting this name 99 times after the morning prayer enlightens the day; 66 times after the morning and evening prayers, Allāh beautifies the reciter's words and actions; 100 times after each of the 5 daily prayers, Allāh counts that person among His devout servants who will be loved and served by all people and every living creature.

Al-Ḥamīd is the All-Praised, the One Who is entitled to all praise and whatever it concerns. He is He Who is the Praised for everything that exists, and for every human being. So let the exceeding of all praise be to Allāh alone.

الله الله الله

أَلْحَيُّ

Al-Ḥayy

The Alive

Exalted and Glorious

Allah, there is no god other than Him, the Ever-Living (*al-Ḥayy*), the Self-Subsisting (*al-Qayyūm*) ... His *kursī* extends over the heavens and the earth, and He feels no fatigue in guarding and preserving. And He is the Most High, the Sublime (*al-ʻaḏẖīm*). (2:255)

Allāh! *Lā ʾilāhaʾillā-huwa* (none has the right to be worshiped, but He), *al-Ḥayyul-Qayyūm* (the Ever Living, the One Who sustains and protects all that exists). (3:2)

And all faces shall be humbled before Allāh, the Ever-Living, the One Who sustains and protects all that exists. And he who carried wrongdoing will be indeed a complete failure on that Day. (20:111)

And put your trust in the Living One Who dies not, and extol His Praise, and Sufficient is He as the All-Knower of the sins of His worshippers. (25:58)

He is the Ever-Living, *Lā ʾ ilāhaʾillā-huwa* (none has the right to be worshiped but He); so invoke Him, making your worship pure for Him Alone. All the praises and thanks be to Allāh, the Lord of the ʻ*Alamin* (mankind, jinn, and all that exists). (40:65)

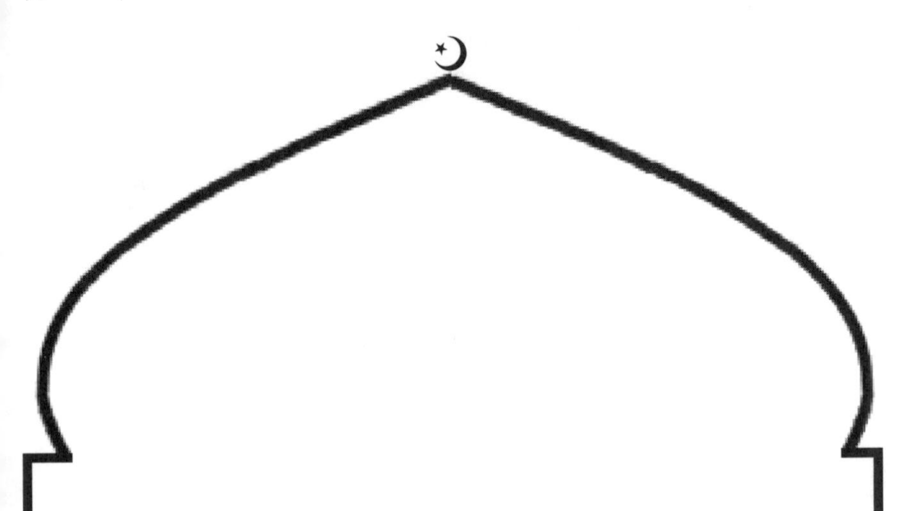

This name means the Ever-Living, the Deathless, the Eternal, His existence having neither beginning nor end. Allāh is the only One Who is Eternal and shall remain forever. He knows, hears and sees all our good and evil intentions and deeds, and has warned of punishments for vicious and sinful acts.

Allāh, the Most High, has neither a partner nor an equal. He has no figure, no form, no color, and no parts.

One who repeats this name one hundred and one times will have long life. Reciting this name 500 times every day before sunrise may bring peace to the stressed or disturbed.

Al-Ḥayy is the Living Purifier of life from the beginning without any beginning or ending. He is the Subsister forever from the world of pre-eternity, and the Ever-Living Who does not die. *Al-Ḥayy* is the One Who distinguishes to you that Allāh is He Who is longed for in every annihilation in your surrender to all His orders.

الله الله الله

أَلْقَيُّومُ

Al-Qayyūm

The Self-Subsisting
Exalted and Glorious

Allāh! *Lā ilāha'illa-huwa* (none has the right to be worshiped, but He), *Al-Ḥayyul-Qayyūm* (the Ever Living, the One Who sustains and protects all that exists). (3:2)

Allāh! *Lā ilāha'illa-huwa* (none has the right to be worshiped, but He) Neither slumber nor sleep overtakes Him. To Him belongs whatever is in the heavens and whatever is on earth. (2:255)

And (all) faces shall be humbled before (Allāh) the Ever-Living. And he who carried wrongdoing will be indeed a complete failure on that Day. (20:111)

This name is an attribute of Allāh meaning the Self-Subsisting. He doesn't depend on anything, nor does He require any support. He is the Omnipotent, Creator and Sustainer of all things. He is the Almighty and the Sole Provider. Allāh sustains the existence of everything.

One who repeats this name ninety-nine times will never fall into hard times.

Al-Qayyūm, the Self-Subsistent Everlasting One Who is perfect in Himself. The One Who stands alone. He is the One Who draws out the origins and provisions of all things through the truth of His created Order, and He is the Knower of their capacities. So let all your thirsting, knowing, and trusting be to Him Who is the Everlasting Order.

الله الله الله

ألْوَاحِدُ

Al-Wāḥid

The One

Exalted and Glorious

And your God (*Ilāh*) is One God – Allāh, *Lā ilāha'illa-huwa* (none has the right to be worshiped, but He), the Most Gracious, the Most Merciful. (2:163)

Say not: "Three! Cease! It is better for you. For Allāh is the Only One God, glory be to Him: (Far Exalted is He) above having a son." (4:171)

Surely, disbelievers are those who said, "Allāh is the third of the three." But there is no god but One God. (5:73)

Can you verily bear witness that besides Allāh there are other gods. Say: "I bear no such witness!" Say: "But in truth He is the Only One God. And truly I am innocent of what you join in worship with Him." (6:19)

Say: "Allāh is the Creator of all things, and He is the One, the Irresistible." (13:16)

Your God is One God. But for those who believe not in the Hereafter, their hearts deny, and they are proud. (16:22)

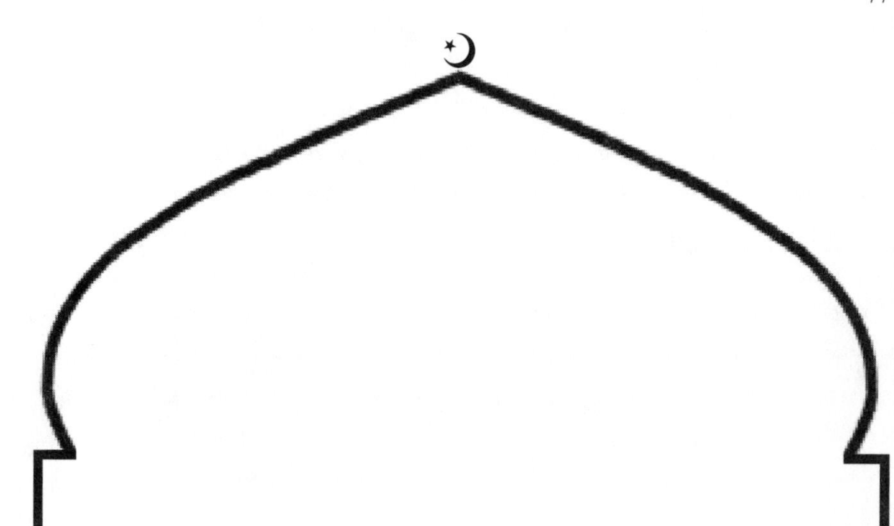

This name clearly reveals that Allāh is the Only One to be worshiped, the Only One having neither beginning nor end, the Only One who is the Eternal and shall remain forever, and the Only One who is the Omnipotent.

Allāh is the Only One to be feared, obeyed, loved, adored and worshiped by all.

If you repeat this name alone and in a quiet place one hundred and thirteen times, you will be free from fear and delusion if God, the Most High wills.

الله الله الله

Al-Āhad

The One

Exalted and Glorious

Say: "He is Allāh, the One." (112:1)

This name is a name of Allāh, synonymous to the previous name, with slight difference and more emphasis on the unity; hence it is more specific and reserved for Allāh only.

He who repeats this name one thousand times, the secret of the universe will be opened to him. By reciting this sacred name of Allāh, there is peace and contentment as well as divine blessings.

Al-Wahid, Al-Ahad – He is One. He is the Singing of the Singer in His essence, in His purity, and in His actions. He is the Determiner of Death in His dominion which no one can take away. He has no partner, glory be to Him. So stand up in the unity of Allāh, and in the perfecting of His Oneness, and be blameless in praising and thanking Him, and of fleeing from reproof.

الله الله الله

أَلصَّمَدُ

Aṣ-Ṣamad

The Eternal
Exalted and Glorious

Allāh-uṣ-Ṣamad, Allāh, the Self-Sufficient Master, Whom all creatures need. (112:2)

This is a name from the names of Allāh meaning that He is free from all the wants and needs of living creatures necessary for performing their normal functions of life such – as eating and drinking. Allāh is Omnipotent, Omniscient, All-Powerful, Complete and Perfect in every respect, and all His attributes are beyond description and imagination. He is not in need of anything, or of any duty from any being or creature for Himself. It is the entire universe and all the creatures living within that need His commands, awards and blessings.

Allāh is the Only Being to appeal to if one has any need to be fulfilled or any trouble to be eliminated.

He who repeats this name frequently one-hundred-nineteen times, Allāh will provide for his needs and as a result, he will not need others, but they will need Him.

Aṣ-Ṣamad is the One Who is Obedient with the command of His order which proceeds immediately to Him in whatever is necessary. He is the Destination towards which His slave is preoccupied both in his religion and in the material world. So do not ask for protection from anyone nor of anything that passes away. Ask for protection only from Him.

الله الله الله

Al-Qādir

The Able

Exalted and Glorious

Say: "Allāh is certainly Able to send down a sign, but most of them know not." (6:37)

Say: "He has power to send torment on you from above and from under your feet, or to cover you with confusion." (6:65)

See they not that Allāh, who created the heavens and the earth, is Able to create the like of them. And He has decreed for them an appointed term, whereof there is no doubt. (17:99)

Is not He Who created the heavens and the earth, Able to create the like of them? Yes, indeed! He is the All-Knowing, Supreme Creator. (36:81)

This name is an attribute of Allāh which manifests His Infinite Ability. He is Almighty. If He wills, He can raise the dead, make stones talk, and trees walk. His power is eternal. He is the First and the Last. He is before everything and after everything. He is not after His essence. He who recites this name one hundred and fourteen times, all his desires will be fulfilled. If a believer recites this name while making ablution, it gives strength to each of the parts or members he is purifying.

الله الله الله

Al-Muqtadir

The Powerful
Exalted and Glorious

And We put forward to them the example of the life of this world. It is like the water which We send down from the sky, and the vegetation of the earth mingles with it, and becomes fresh and green, but later it becomes dry and broken pieces, which the winds scatter: And Allāh is Able to do everything. (18:45)

They belied all Our Signs, so We seized them with a Seizure of the All-Mighty, All-Capable. (54:42)

This name is an attribute of Allāh which is synonymous with the previous name *al-Qādir*.

Allāh has power over everything. He gives life and also death. It is by His Command that everything changes. He who repeats this name five-hundred times will be aware of the truth.

Al-Muqtadir is He Who destines the goodly characteristics of His face. There is no Capable One better nor other than He. So if you feel inadequate in realizing the orders of Allāh, then change all your endeavors to be only your returning to Him.

الله الله الله

He is the First (nothing is before Him) and the Last (nothing is after Him), the Most High (nothing is above Him) and the Most Near (nothing is nearer than Him), and He is the All-Knower of every thing. (57:3)

This name is another attribute of Allāh that reveals and establishes His Being prior to and before anything.

He who would like to have a child but cannot or has a beloved person missing or has any over-whelming problem, if he repeats this name one thousand times for forty Fridays, his desires will be fulfilled if Allāh, the Most High wills. *Ya ʾAwwal*

Al-ʾAwwal, the First. He is the One Whom nothing preceded in His existence. He was the First before existence. So believe in Him, and assert that He is the First of every manifest and unmanifest thing. And there is nothing else with Him ever.

الله الله الله

أَلآخِرُ

Al-ʾĀkẖir

The Last

Exalted and Glorious

He is the First (nothing is before Him) and the Last (nothing is after Him), the Most High (nothing is above Him) and the Most Near (nothing is nearer than Him), and He is the All-Knower of every thing. (57:3)

This attribute of Allāh reveals that He will remain forever even after everything is annihilated.

There will be an end to all thoughts, intentions, and knowledge, but He is Final and Perfect in every respect. This name is always accompanied by the previous one, and he who repeats this name six-hundred times frequently will not only lead a happy life in this world, but will also have a happy ending.

Al-ʾĀkẖir, the Last is the One Who subsists in everlasting subsistence after the annihilation of His creation in His everlasting subsistence. He is the Enricher of all subsistence, both present and in all time because nothing is after Him. You should know that your belief is in bearing witness that Allāh is the Eternal Subsister Who is the basis of all surrendered belief.

الله الله الله

Aḍẖ-Ḍẖāhir

The Manifest

Exalted and Glorious

He is the First (nothing is before Him) and the Last (nothing is after Him), the Manifest (*aḍẖ-ḍẖāhir*) and the concealed (*al-bāṭin*), and He is the All-Knower of every thing. (57:3)

This name is an attribute of Allāh meaning the Manifest. Allāh's signs are evident everywhere in the universe. Allāh is the Manifest and nothing is hidden from Him. His knowledge not only comprehends all things, but has all things actively before it. Allāh's All-Embracing Knowledge is independent of time, place, or circumstances.

He who recites this name fifteen times every other Friday prayer, the divine light will enter his heart. Reciting this name enables one to see things which were previously hidden. If someone has a difficulty and no idea how to find a solution he may, after his night prayer, do two rakats of prayer and recite *Ya Ḍẖahir* 1006 times asking God to show him the solution of his problem. The solution may be shown in his dreams.

Aḍẖ-Ḍẖahir is the Revealed Who is the Manifest One above everything and to everything. He is the Manifest of His existence in His many proofs. So let us be aware of the signs of Allāh, the Manifest in His essence and in all created beings.

الله الله الله

أَلْبَاطِنُ

Al-Bāṭin

The Hidden

Exalted and Glorious

He is the First (nothing is before Him) and the Last (nothing is after Him), the Manifest (*adẖ-ḍẖāhir*) and the concealed (*al-bāṭin*), and He is the All-Knower of every thing. (57:3)

One of His ninety-nine names is Allāh, the Hidden One, or the Concealed One, or He Who Knows Hidden Things.

Allāh's signs are everywhere evident in the whole universe. This pair of seemingly opposite qualities, the First and the Last, the Evident and the Immanent, are referred here to reveal the contrast without human frailty.

He who repeats this name three times every day will be able to see the truth in things.

Al-Bāṭin is the Hidden One. He is the Knower in His hiddenness, in His orders, and in His secret, Who appears in the material world and shows you His influences. So let your remembrance of Him in the hidden be in the overwhelming of your self, and in being aware of your incapacity for which you must purify your inner being.

الله الله الله

Al-Wāliy

The Governor
Exalted and Glorious

Know you not that it is Allāh to Whom belongs the dominion of the heavens and the earth? And besides Allāh you have neither any *Wāliy* nor helper. (2:107)

And if you were to follow their desires after what you have received of Knowledge, then you would have against Allāh neither any *Wāliy* nor any helper. (2:120)

Verily, among mankind who have the best claim to ᵓIbrāhīm are those who followed him, and this Prophet (*ṣala-llāhu ᶜalayhi wa sallim*), and those who have believed. And Allāh is *Wāliy* of the believers. (3:68)

But remind them with it lest a person be given up to destruction for that which he has earned, when he will find for himself no protector or intercessor besides Allāh. (6:70)

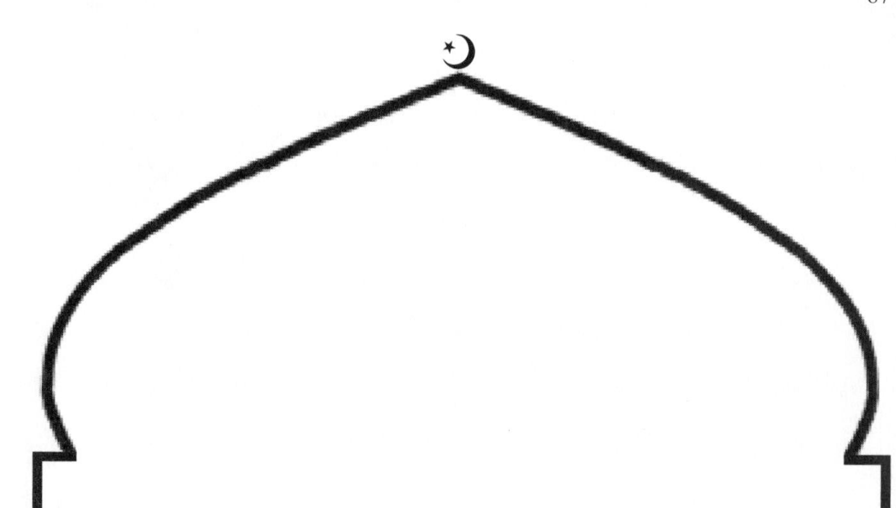

This attribute clearly indicates that it is Allāh Who directs, manages, governs and measures. Allāh has appointed guardians to accompany His bondsmen to keep a full record of all deeds.

He who repeats this name thirty-three times and breathes it into his house, his house will be free from danger.

Al-Wāliy is the Friend Who is the King of all things, the Administrator and the Judge before Whom all is witnessed, and Who carries out His orders, and the One to Whom His order returns. So be the watcher over your condition, and know that whatever mistakes you are given are for the strengthening of whatever you have achieved.

الله الله الله

All-Knower of the Unseen and the Seen, the Most Great, the Most High. (13:9)

This name is one of the ninety-nine names of Allāh, the Most Great, the Most High, the Lofty One.

He who repeats this name frequently will gain the benevolence of Allāh. Recitation of this sacred name of Allāh restores lost capabilities, power, and prestige. Say: My Lord, increase me in knowledge.

Al-Muta^cāli is the Exalted Who is not preceded by anything in existence. He is the Exalted before all existence. So let us believe with a belief of absolute certainty that Allāh is the Exalted One without anything else being with Him in this.

الله الله الله

Al-Barr

The Source of All Goodness
Exalted and Glorious

Verily, We used to invoke Him (Alone and none else) before. Verily, He is *al-Barr* (the Most Subtle, Kind, Courteous, and Generous), the Most Merciful. (52:28)

This attribute of Allāh in its ordinary sense means pious or good. As applied to Allāh it means the Beneficent One Who is tolerant toward His servants, toward all creatures and is good to them.

He who repeats this name over a child, this child will be free from misfortune. Parents who lose a child very young should not despair, for Allāh, the Exalted, in all His kindness and mercy shall bless them with children who survive if they profusely recite this sacred name.

Al-Barr is the Beneficent Who is favorably disposed towards His slaves through His blamelessness and His subtlety. He is Gracious to those who ask of Him for His beautiful bestowing. He is the Truthful One in what He promises. So let us ask Allāh for His blamelessness and His subtlety that in His good pleasure He may accept us.

الله الله الله

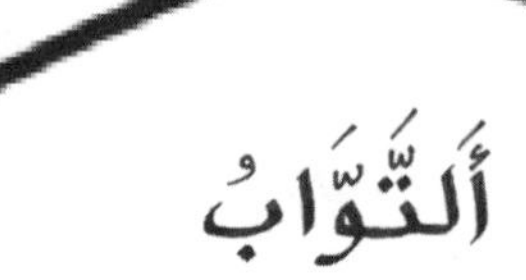

At-Tawwāb

The Accepter of Repentance
Exalted and Glorious

So turn (in repentance) to your Creator, and mortify your selves. That will be better for you with your Creator. Then He accepted your repentance. Truly, He is the One Who accepts repentance, the Most Merciful. (2:54)

And had it not been for the Grace of Allāh and His Mercy on you. And that Allāh is the One Who forgives and accepts repentance, the All-Wise. (24:10)

Would one of you like to eat the flesh of his dead brother? You would hate it (so hate backbiting). And fear Allāh. Verily, Allāh is the One Who forgives and accepts repentance, Most Merciful. (49:12)

– also see sūratu-t-tawbah (9)

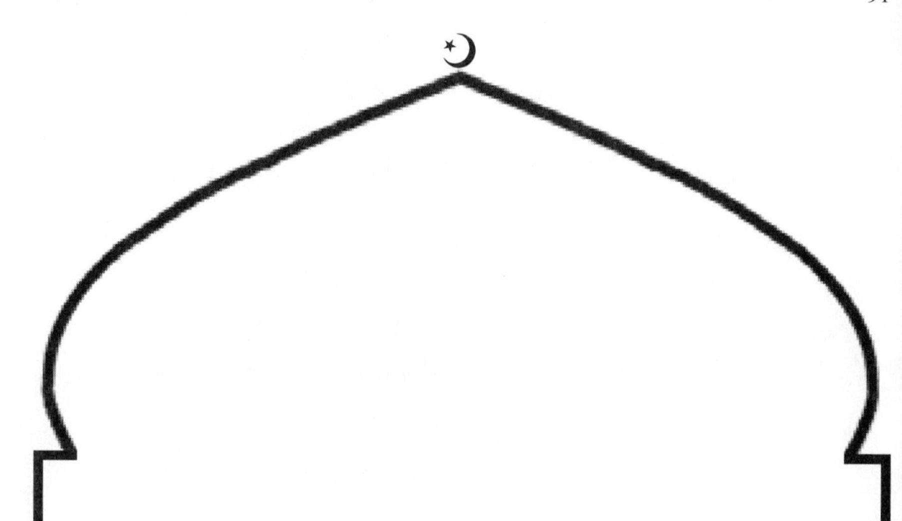

When they were unjust to themselves, if they had only come to the Prophet, *ṣala-llāhu ᶜalayhi wa sallim* and asked Allāh's forgiveness, and the Prophet, *ṣala-llāhu ᶜalayhi wa sallim* had asked forgiveness for them, they would have found Allāh indeed to be the One Who accepts repentance, the Most Merciful. According to Islamic *Shari'ah,* the validity of repentance depends on three things: a confession of one's sins, remorse, and a firm resolution to abstain from its recurrence.

He who repeats this name frequently, his repentance will be accepted.

At-Tawwāb is the One Who accepts the repentance of His slaves when He turns to them and receives their repentance and their returning to Him. He is the One Who constantly forgives sins and wrongdoings as they perish in Him. So let us return to Him in all our affairs.

الله الله الله

Al-ᶜAfūww

The Pardoner
Exalted and Glorious

Or you have been in contact with women (by sexual relations), and you find no water, perform *tayammum** with clean earth and rub therewith your faces and hands. Truly, Allāh is Ever Oft-Pardoning, Oft-Forgiving. (4:43)

These are they whom Allāh is likely to forgive, and Allāh is Ever Oft-Pardoning, Oft-Forgiving. (4:99)

None can be their mothers except those who gave them birth. And verily, Allāh is Oft-Pardoning, Oft-Forgiving. (58:2)

---

*When you strike your hands on the earth, then pass the palm of each on the back of the other, then blow off the dust from them, and then pass or rub them on your face, this is called *tayammum.*

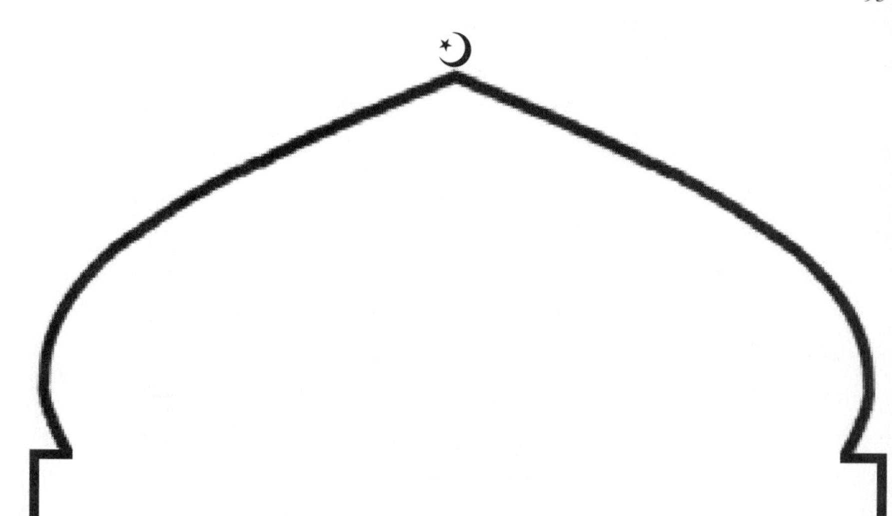

This name is another attribute of Allāh which means One Who pardons or cancels, the Pardoner (of sins). Allāh pardons all who repent sincerely as if they had no previous sins.

He who repeats this name frequently, and after that prays, "Oh Allāh, You are the Forgiver and You like to forgive, I pray for You to forgive my sins," Allāh, the All-Mighty will forgive all his sins.

Al-ᶜAfūww is the Forgiver Who relieves the torment of wrongdoings, shortcomings, and deficiencies in His erasing of them. He is at enmity with disobedience, but do not despair of His Favor and Forgiveness towards your sins because Allāh Himself is your Forgiver.

الله الله الله

ألرَّؤُوف

Ar-Raʾūf

The Compassionate, the Clement
Exalted and Glorious

And Allāh would never make your faith (prayer) to be lost. Truly, Allāh is full of Kindness, the Most Merciful towards mankind. (2:143)

And of mankind is he who would sell himself, seeking the Pleasure of Allāh. And Allāh is full of Kindness to His slaves. (2:207)

And Allāh warns you against Himself (His Punishment). And Allāh is full of Kindness to His slaves. (3:30)

After that the hearts of a party of them had nearly deviated (from the Right Path), but He accepted their repentance. Certainly, He is unto them full of Kindness, Most Merciful. (9:117)

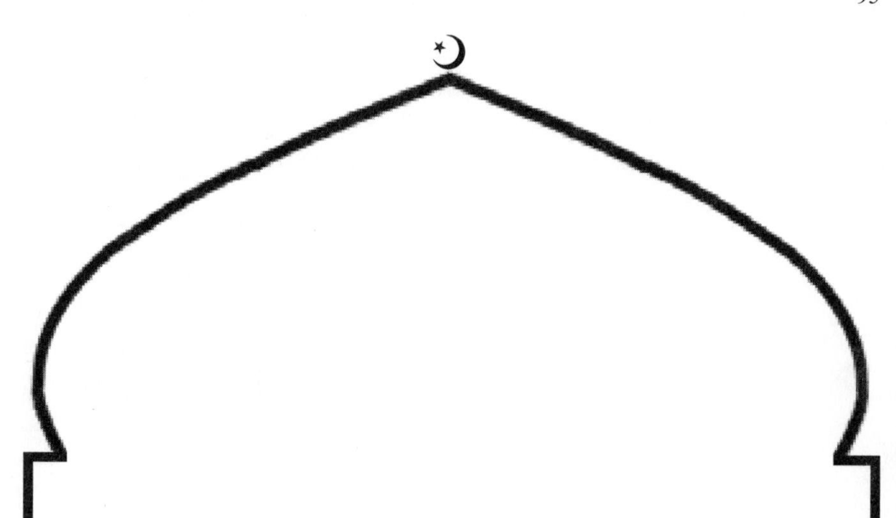

This name is an attribute of Allāh which means the compassionate. Allāh is full of kindness and mercy. His blessing keeps His purity spotless, for He hears all prayer and knows all the temptations to which human nature is subject.

He who repeats this name frequently will be blessed by Allāh. The recitation of this sacred name of Allāh turns a harsh and hard master into a kind and lenient one.

Ar-Raʾūf is the Gentle One Who through His Forgiveness is favorably disposed towards sinners. He is the Generous in His Subtlety and Gentleness, and in His Compassion, covers over your defects and then forgives them. So worship Him in what He confirms in you in your standing up to struggle in obedience to Him, glory be to Him.

الله الله الله

> Surely, Allāh will collect the hypocrites and disbelievers all together in Hell. (4:140)

> Our Lord! Verily, it is You Who will gather mankind together on the Day about which there is no doubt. Verily, Allāh never breaks His Promise. (3:9)

Allāh is One who collects things and gathers them anywhere He wants at anytime.

He who repeats this name will find the things that he has lost. One who has been separated from his people, family or friends, may recite this sacred name of Allāh 114 times, and He in all His kindness and mercy shall reunite them. This is followed by, "*Ya Jām*ᶜ*i an-nasi li-yawmin la rayba fiyhi ijma' 'alayya dalati* – O Gatherer of humanity for the day about which their is no doubt, bring what I have lost together with me!"

*Al- Jām*ᶜ*i* is the Gatherer Together. It is Allāh Who gathers together all perfection of essence, qualities, and deeds. It is He Who unites all varying characteristics as He wishes. It is He Who will bring together the 'first ones' and the 'last ones' in the One Master. So knowing that Allāh will gather you together on the Day of Reckoning, be prepared for that Day.

الله الله الله

Al-Gẖaniyy

The Self-Sufficient, the Rich One
Exalted and Glorious

And Lord is Rich (Self-Sufficient), full of Mercy; if He wills, He can destroy you, and in your place make whom He wills as your successors. (6:133)

They say: "Allāh has begotten a son!" Glory is to Him! He is Rich (Free of all needs)! His is all that is in the heavens and all that is in the earth. (10:68)

Oh mankind! it is you who stand in need of Allāh. But Allāh is Rich, Worthy of all praise. (35:15)

This attribute of Allāh expresses the superiority of the Almighty over the necessities and requirements of mankind. Man needs Allāh and depends on Him all his life.

He who repeats this name will be contented and will not be envious. If the ones who are in material need recite this name 1060 times on Saturdays, they will not need the help of others.

Al-Gẖaniyy is the All-Rich. He Who does not dispute about anything is the Rich One above all else to Whom all who are needy come running. If you know that Allāh is the only All-Rich, then do not ask of any other than He.

الله الله الله

An-Nūr

The Light
Exalted and Glorious

Indeed, there has come to you from Allāh a light, and a plain Book. (5:15)

So those who believe in him (Muhammad, *ṣala-llāhu ᶜalayhi wa sallim*), honor him, help him, and follow the light which has been sent down with him. (7:157)

They want to extinguish Allāh's Light with their mouths, but Allāh will not allow except that His Light should be perfected, even though the disbelievers hate it. (9:32)

Allāh is the Light of the heavens and the earth. (24:35)
(This is known as the Chapter of Divine Light.)

They intend to put out the Light of Allāh with their mouths. But Allāh will bring His Light to perfection even though the disbelievers hate it. (61:8)

This attribute of Allāh clearly indicates that Allāh, the Most High is the Only Reality as He is the Only Light.

The Messenger of Allāh, may Allāh's peace and blessings be upon him, says, "God has seventy-thousand veils of light." Gabriel says, "Between me and Him are seventy-thousand veils of Light."

As all our lights have their source in the Primary Light, the One Reality, there can be no light unless Allāh gives the light. He who repeats this name will have inner light.

If believers find their hearts dark with doubt and sadness and read *Surah Nūr* 7 times and recite this name 1000 times, they will find their doubts eliminated and their hearts enlightened.

An-Nūr is the Light of the Guide of Righteousness Who reveals the right way, through His guidance, to whomever He wishes, and to whomever He makes clear His truth. He fills him with yearning by His imprinting on him the purifying of his essence and the cleansing of his zeal. So let us be enlightened in His righteousness through His guidance.

الله الله الله

أَلْهَادِيُ

Al-Hādiy

The Guide

Exalted and Glorious

Thus have We made for every Prophet an enemy among the *mujrimun* (disbelievers). But Sufficient is your Lord as a Guide and Helper. (25:31)

This name is an attribute of Allāh of guidance to the right path. This guidance pours forth as the guidance of Allāh for all the creation, including minerals, plants, and animals; the guidance from Allāh, which was preached by His Messenger to their followers; the guidance from Allāh, which may be defined as divine help; and the divine guidance by which the righteous believers shall attain their salvation in the Hereafter.

Allāh imparts wisdom to His faithful servants and guides them to the right path, but sinners, liars, infidels and swindlers are debarred from the guidance. He who recites this name will gain spiritual knowledge.

'Abdul Hādiy is the servant of Allāh who has received the response to his prayer – Guide us on the right path. Recitation of this name 200 times a day may lead to success.

Al-Hādiy is the Guide Who is Clear Evidence of the Path of the Truth. His words guide hearts to the knowledge of His essence, and selves to His obedience and the manifestation of His attributes. There is no guidance except that of Allāh through the revelation of His book and His Messenger, the prayers and peace of Allāh be upon him.

الله الله الله

Al-Badī^{c}

The Originator
Exalted and Glorious

> The Originator of the heavens and the earth. When He decrees a matter, He only says to it: “Be!” – and it is. (2:117)

> He is the Originator of the heavens and the earth. How can He have children when He has no wife? He created all things, and He is the All-Knower of everything. (6:101)

This name is an attribute of Allāh meaning, He Who Originates. Allāh created this world with what it contains of beauty. *Ya Badī^{c} as-samawati wal-ard.*

He who repeats this name seventy times saying, “Oh He Who is the Originator of incomparable things in the heavens and on the earth,” all his troubles will disappear. Reciting this name of Allāh is invaluable for the accomplishment of a difficult task or for the attainment of a difficult objective.

Al-Badī^{c} is the Originator Who has no likeness in His purity or judgment. There is no order like His order because He is the One Who is Ever-New in existence without any other likeness. So my Muslim brother, contemplate the origin of your calling, and what has been laid down for you until your faith is firmly established.

الله الله الله

Ar-Rabb

The Sustainer

Exalted and Glorious

All the praises and thanks be to Allāh, *Rabb al-^{c}Alamin* (the Lord of the worlds – mankind, *jinn*, and all that exists). (1:2)

He said: "Oh my Lord! I have power only over myself and my brother, so separate us from the people who are the *fasiqun* (rebellious and disobedient to Allāh)!" (5:25)

So the root of the people who did wrong was cut off. And all the praise and thanks are to Allāh, *Rabb al-^{c}Alamin* (the Lord of the worlds – mankind, *jinn*, and all that exists). (6:45)

Say: "Verily, my *salat*, my sacrifice, my living, and my dying are for Allāh, the Lord of the ^{c}*Alamin*, (the Lord of the worlds – mankind, *jinn*, and all that exists)." (6:162)

And remember when ʾIbrāhīm said: "My Lord, make this city (Mecca) a place of security and provide its people with fruits, such of them as believe in Allāh and the Last Day." (2:126)

This name is an attribute of Him Who watches, guides, and sustains that which is in His care. Allāh is the Lord of all in the universe. By reciting this Divine Name, as many times as possible, ways and means open up for the best possible way of bringing up children. Reciting this name is also a safety against dangers of all kinds.

الله الله الله

أَلْمُبِينُ

Al-Mubīn

The Manifest

Exalted and Glorious

On that day Allāh will pay them the recompense of their deeds in full, and they will know that Allāh, He is the Manifest Truth. (24:25)

This attribute of Allāh is the True Light of which all physical light is merely a type or a kind.

Allāh witnesses what is done on this earth, and nothing is hidden from Him. His knowledge has a quality which human knowledge has no knowledge of. Human knowledge is subject to time and is obliterated by time. God's knowledge is like a record and endures forever. And His record has a quality which human records do not have.

Allāh's all watchful knowledge and care over all His creatures may be a source of fear to the unbeliever, but there is no fear for those whom He honors with His love, neither in this world nor in the world to come.

الله الله الله

ٱلْقَدِيرُ

Al-Qadīr

The Mighty
Exalted and Glorious

The lightning almost snatches away their sight, whenever it flashes for them, they walk therein, and when darkness covers them, they stand still. And if Allāh willed, He could have taken away their hearing and their sight. Certainly, Allāh has Power over all things. (2:20)

Know you not that God has Power over all things? (2:106)

You endue with honor whom You will, and You humiliate whom You will. Verily, You are Able to do all things. (3:26)

And Allāh is All-Powerful, All-Wise. (5:38)

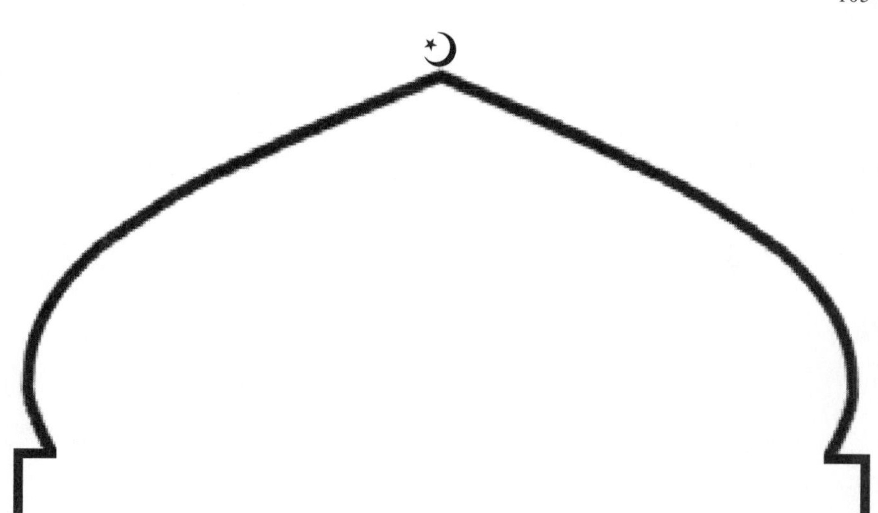

This is an attribute of Allāh which means the Mighty. Allāh has full power over everything in this world, even over our life and death. No other creature has any power that Allāh's might does not dominate.

While performing ablution, if one keeps reciting this name of Allāh, it will bring him ascendancy over his foes and freedom from dangers.

Al-Qadīr is the All-Powerful Who decrees His wisdom to everything that is existent and non-existent. Its decree is not apparent, and does not provide for it, and does not inform accurately of it, but Allāh is the All-Aware of all the decrees, and determines their wisdom and their organization. So let us surrender ourselves to His judgment in everything, because everything is made by the hand of the power of Allāh.

الله الله الله

أَلْحَافِظُ

Al-Ḥāfiḍẖ

The Protector
Exalted and Glorious

Allāh is the best Protector, and He is the most Merciful of those who show mercy. (12:64)

Verily, We, it is We Who have sent down the Qur'an and surely, We will Guard it (from corruption). (15:9)

This name is another attribute which means the Protector. All creatures are protected by Allāh in many ways that they do not even know. Allāh is also the Guardian of the Holy Qur'an. The Holy Qur'an is the Word of Allāh and He preserves it. None can do harm to it, or discredit it by his ridiculous taunts and objections.

By repeating this name of Allāh, and wearing it written on something you are wearing, calamities are kept away.

This is *Ḥāfiḍẖ*. The letter 'ā' is *alif* in Arabic and this means He is *al-Ḥāfiḍẖ* Who is the Protector of *al-Qurʾān*. This name is different from *al-Ḥafiḍẖ,* meaning the Lord Preserver of and above all the worlds, which was mentioned earlier, in which the letter 'a' in *Ḥafiḍẖ* is a vowel in Arabic.

الله الله الله

أَلْكَفِيلُ

Al-Kafīl

The Surety

Exalted and Glorious

And fulfill the covenant of Allāh when you have made a covenant with Him, and break not your oaths after you have confirmed them – and indeed you have appointed Allāh your surety. (16:91)

This name is one attribute of Allāh which means the Surety. Allāh is the Witness of the True Ever-Living God. He is everywhere and is always with us.

Reciting this sacred name of Allāh twenty-one times every morning instills good manners and good morals in children.

الله الله الله

أَلشَّاكِرُ

Ash-Shākir

The Appreciative
Exalted and Glorious

And whoever does good voluntarily, then verily Allāh is All-Appreciative, All-Knower. (2:158)

Why should Allāh punish you if you have thanked Him and have believed in Him. And Allāh is Ever All-Appreciative, All-Knowing. (4:147)

Allāh does not like that the evil should be uttered in public except by him who has been wronged. And Allāh is ever All-Hearer, All-Knower. (4:148)

This name is still another attribute of Allāh Who appreciates and recognizes any good which He finds in us. Through this auspicious name, Allāh has invaluable blessing for those whose means of livelihood is limited. When such people recite this sacred name every day forty-one times over a cup of water, and rub it on their breast and eyes, there will be a change for the better and troubles will diminish. *Ash-Shakūr*, mentioned before is more than *ash-Shākir*.

الله الله الله

Read! And your Lord is the Most Generous. (96:3)

This attribute of Allāh means the Most Bounteous, Most Generous. Allāh sustains all the creation and bestows His favors upon His servants. It is from the Kindness of Allāh that He revealed the Holy *Qurʾān* for the guidance of mankind.

Allāh has shown grace to the believers by sending the Messenger of Allāh, may the peace and blessings of Allāh be upon him. Allāh exalted His Messenger and conferred upon him the honor of being the Noblest of all men.

Allāh is *al-dẖu-l-jalāli wa-l-ʾikram*, the Lord of Majesty and Honor. He in His holiness is the Purity of Majesty, Honor, and Might. He is the Most Distinguished in nobility and generosity. So let us be as Allāh wants, following the family of Allāh, surrendering in our lives, and manifesting Him in all our states.

الله الله الله

Al-Āᶜla

The Most High

Exalted and Glorious

Glorify the Name of your Lord, the Most High (87:1)

This is another attribute of Allāh which means the Most High. Allāh is the Real King and above all. He is the Most High and Mighty.

When the verse (87:1) was revealed, the Messenger of Allāh, may Allāh's peace and blessings be upon him, said, "Oh you, recite the prayer: 'Glory be to my Lord, the Exalted,' three times during your supplication."

الله الله الله

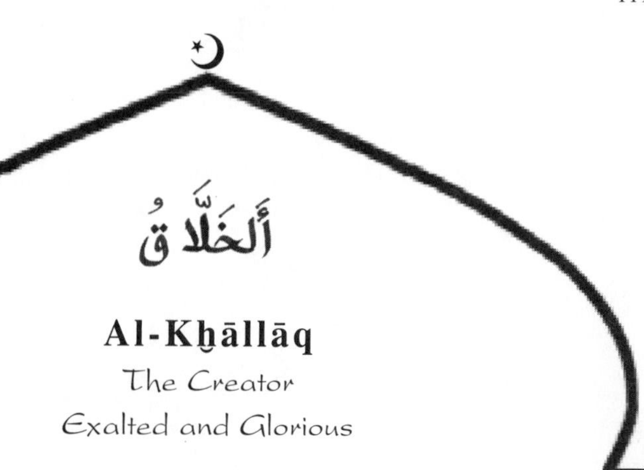

Al-Kẖāllāq

The Creator

Exalted and Glorious

Is not He who created the heavens and the earth able to create the like of them? Yes, indeed! He is the All-Knowing Supreme Creator. (36:81)

Verily, your Lord is the All-Knowing Creator. (15:86)

This name is one of the ninety-nine attributes of Allāh. He is the Creator Who is perfect in His skill and knowledge. This name is different from *al-Kẖāliq,* Who is the Originator of everything, Who is the Maker Creator. *Al-Kẖallāq* is He Who perfects His skill in all the worlds.

Continuous recitation of this name of Allāh in the quiet hours of night is rewarded by continuous blessings until the Day of Reckoning.

الله الله الله

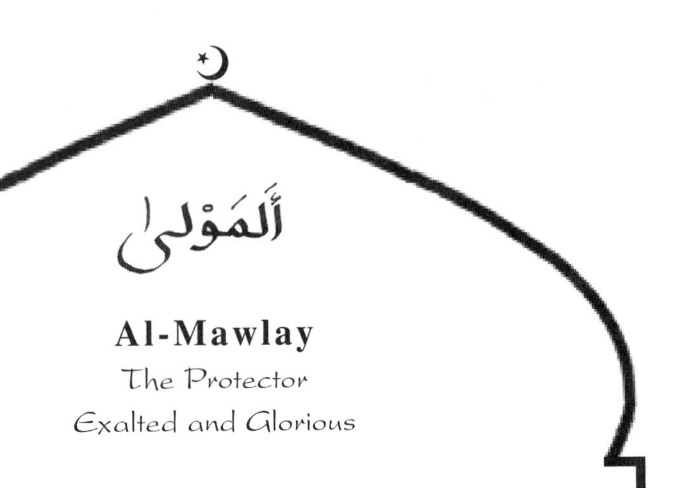

Al-Mawlay

The Protector
Exalted and Glorious

Our Lord! Put not on us a burden greater than we have strength to bear. Pardon us and grant us forgiveness. Have mercy on us. You are our *Mawlay* (Protector), and give us victory over the disbelieving people. (2:286)

And if they turn away, then know that Allāh is your *Mawlay* (Protector), what an excellent *Mawlay*, and what an excellent Helper! (8:40)

That is because Allāh is the *Mawlay* (Protector) of those who believe, and the disbelievers have no *Mawlay*. (47:11)

This name is an attribute of Allāh; we should pray only to Allāh for help only from Him.

الله الله الله

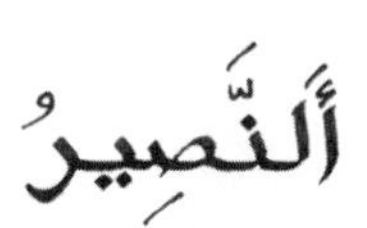

An-Naṣir

The Helper

Exalted and Glorious

Know you not that it is Allāh to Whom belongs the dominion of the heavens and the earth? And besides Allāh you have neither *Wali* nor any helper. (2:107)

And if you were to follow their desires after what you have received of Knowledge, then you would have against Allāh neither any *Waliy* nor any helper. (2:120)

They are those whom Allāh has cursed, and he whom Allāh curses, you will not find for him any helper. (4:52)

But if they turn away Allāh will punish them with a painful torment in this worldly life and in the Hereafter. And there is none for them on earth as a *Waliy* or a helper. (9:74)

Say: "My Lord! Let my entry be good and likewise my exit be good. And grant me from You an authority to help me." (17:80)

This name is an attribute of Allāh which means the Helper. Allāh's help gives satisfaction and contentment to those who believe, as they bear the difficulties of the world with courage.

Anas narrated that when the Messenger of Allāh, may the peace and blessings of Allāh be upon him, went forth to battle, he would say, "Oh Allāh! You are my Arm and my Helper. With Your help, do I move, with Your Help do I assail, and with Your help do I battle."

الله الله الله

Al-Llāh

The God

Exalted and Glorious

Were you witnesses when death approached Ya'qub? When he said unto his sons, "What will you worship after me?" They said: "We shall worship your *Ilāh* (God), the *Ilāh* of your fathers Ibrahim, Isma'il, and Ishaq, One *Ilāh* and to Him we submit." (2:133)

And your god is One God: There is no god but He, Most Gracious, Most Merciful. (2:163)

No son did Allāh beget, nor is there any god (*ilāh*) along with Him. (If there had been many gods), then each god would have taken away what he had created, and some would have tried to overcome others! (23:91)

Say: "It is revealed to me that your *Ilāh* (God) is only one *Ilāh*." (21:108)

The name Allāh is the essential name of God. Allāh is One. He has no partner with Him. This name, *Llāh* is considered an attribute of the Divine Being. The Supreme Name, Allāh is distinguished from everything and also from His attribute *Al-Ilāh* whose meaning can be understood in the saying: "There is no god, but the God and He is One God."

الله الله الله

أَلْقَاهِرُ

Al-Qāhir

The Omnipotent
Exalted and Glorious

He is the Irresistible (Supreme) over His slaves, and He sends guardians over you, until when death approaches one of you, Our messengers take his soul, and they never neglect their duty. (6:61)

He is the Omnipotent over His slaves, and He is the Wise, the Knower. (6:18)

This name is an attribute of Allāh which means the Omnipotent, the All-Mighty. Allāh holds dominance over all His creatures, and no one can reach to His power and excellence.

Continuous recitation of this name gives protection against the temptations of this world.

الله الله الله

أَلْغَافِرُ

Al-Gẖāfir

The Forgiver
Exalted and Glorious

You are our Protector; so forgive us and have mercy on us. You are the Best of those who forgive. (7:155)

The Forgiver of sin, the Accepter of repentance, the Severe in punishment, the Bestower of favors. *Lā ᵓilāhaᵓilla ḥuwa* (none has the right to be worshiped, but He). To Him is the final return. (40:3)

This name of Allāh is another attribute of Allāh which means that He is the Forgiver. *Al-Gẖaffūr* is the Forgiver of all things everywhere; *Al-Gẖāfir* is the Forgiver for anyone, the Forgiver of the recipient. Allāh is the Supreme and He is All-Reaching. He forgives our sins and accepts our repentance when it is sincere. On the other hand, Allāh is strict in punishment.

الله الله الله

Al-ᶜAllām

The Omniscient
Exalted and Glorious

Know they not that Allāh knows their secret ideas, and their *najwa* (secret counsels) and that Allāh is the All-Knower of things unseen? (9:78)

Say: "Verily my Lord sends down the Truth, the All-Knower of the *Ghaib* (Unseen)." (34:48)

On the day when Allāh will gather together the messengers, and say to them, "What was the response you received?" They will say, "We have no knowledge, verily, only You are the All-Knower of all that is hidden." (5:109)

This name is an attribute of Allāh which means the Omniscient, the All-Knowing. Allāh knows all about His creatures and nothing is hidden from Him.

The Messenger of Allāh, may the peace and blessings of Allāh be upon him, said, "When anyone wants to do anything, let him pray two prostrations besides the obligatory prayer, then let him say: 'Oh Allāh! Behold, I ask of You the good through Your knowledge, and ability through Your power, and beg (Your favors) out of Your infinite bounty. For behold, You have power, I have none. You know, I know not. And You are the Great Knower of things hidden.'" (Bukhari)

الله الله الله

Al-Fāṭir

The Creator

Exalted and Glorious

Say: "Shall I take for a *Waliy* (Helper, Protector) any other than Allāh, the Creator (Maker) of the heavens and the earth?" (6:14)

Oh my Lord! You have indeed bestowed on me of the sovereignty, and taught me something of the interpretation of dreams – the (Only) Creator of the heavens and the earth! (12:101)

Their Messengers said: "What! Can there be a doubt about Allāh, the Creator of the heavens and the earth?" (14:10)

Say: "Oh Allāh! Creator of the heavens and the earth! All-Knower of the *Ghaib* (Unseen) and the seen! You will judge between Your Slaves about that wherein they used to differ." (39:46)

This name is an attribute of Allāh which means the Creator. Allāh created the heavens and the earth. Allāh as well is perfect and continues to create because He has All-Power and His mercy is overwhelming.

الله الله الله

Al-Malīk

The Sovereign
Exalted and Glorious

In a seat of truth, near the Omnipotent King. (54:55)

This name is an attribute of Allāh which means the Sovereign. Allāh is the First and the Last. He is All-in-All and is present everywhere and at all times.

Reciting this sacred name softens the strains and enhances one's resources.

According to tradition, al-Khidr, *ṣala-llāhu ᶜalayhi wa sallim*, taught the following prayer to be said 100 times over a sick person and if Allāh so wills a healing will follow:

Allahumma antal malik ul-haqq ulladhi lā ᵓilāhaᵓill anta, ya Allāhu, Ya Salamu, Ya Shafi, Ya Shifa al qulub (x3)

Our Allāh, You are the True King, other than whom there is no other god. O Allāh, O Source of peace, O Healer, O Medicine of hearts!

Al-Malik Al-Mulk – Allāh is the Honored One in His Kingdom as He wishes. His wisdom has no limit, nor is there any subsequent order after His. So have humility with a pleading tongue for success, and be needy of what is in His hand.

الله الله الله

Al-Hafiyy

The Most Gracious
Exalted and Glorious

ʾIbrāhīm said, "Peace be on you! I will ask Forgiveness of my Lord for you. Verily He is unto me Ever Most Gracious." (19:47)

This name is an attribute of Allāh which signifies that He is well disposed to, favorable to, and good to His servants. Allāh is the Most and Only Gracious One to His servants.

الله الله الله

أَلْمُحِيطُ

Al-Muḥīṭ

The All-Pervading
Exalted and Glorious

Verily they are in doubt concerning the Meeting with their Lord? Verily! He it is Who is surrounding all things! (41:54)

This name is another attribute of Allāh which means that Allāh is the All-Pervading.

Allāh, the Most-High is close to everything that exists and is with His creatures in their deeds and movements. Some people feel some difficulty when it comes to offering their prayers. Such people should go to sleep with their hands on their bosom after reciting this sacred name of Allāh seven times. They shall find their will and determination strengthened.

الله الله الله

أَلْمُسْتَعَانُ

Al-Mustaᶜān

One Who Is Called Upon For Help
Exalted and Glorious

He said, "My Lord! Judge You in truth, Our Lord is the Most Gracious, Whose help is to be sought against that which you attribute!" (21:112)

This name is an attribute of Allāh meaning the One Who Is Called Upon For Help.

We pray to Allāh, for He is the Lord of the whole universe and He is the Master of everything. We turn for help to Allāh, and we worship Him alone, and we ask only Him for only His aid.

الله الله الله

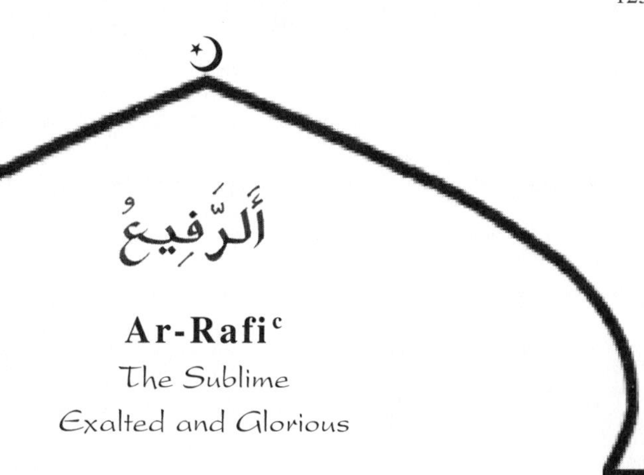

Ar-Rafi[c]

The Sublime
Exalted and Glorious

He is Allāh Owner of High Ranks and Degrees, the Owner of the Throne. He sends the revelation by His Command to any of His slaves He wills, that he may warn of the Day of Mutual Meeting. (40:15)

This name is an attribute of Allāh which means the Sublime. Allāh is above any rank or degree which we can imagine.

He who repeats this name one-hundred times, day and night, Allāh will elevate him higher as far as honor, richness and merit are concerned.

Al-Khafid al-Rafi[c] is the One who abases everyone who is haughty and mighty, and goes beyond the limits of Allāh's law, and is in rebellion. He is the One Who raises His believing slaves through acts of obedience; He is the One Who raises the heavens and the clouds. So have humility, and do not be arrogant. Raise what Allāh has raised by following His commands, and abase what Allāh has abased by following His prohibitions.

الله الله الله

ألكافي

Al-Kāfīy

The Sufficient

Exalted and Glorious

Is not Allāh Sufficient for His slave? Yet they try to frighten you with those besides Him! And whom Allāh sends astray, for him there will be no guide. (39:36)

This name is an attribute of Allāh which means the Sufficient. The righteous man will find Allāh enough for his protection. One should hold fast to Allāh's truth. Then nothing can mislead or betray him.

الله الله الله

أَلْغَالِبُ

Al-Gẖālib

The Predominant
Exalted and Glorious

And Allāh has full power and control over His affairs, but most of men know not. (12:21)

This name is an attribute of Allāh which means the Predominant. Allāh is full of might and majesty and is able to enforce His will.

الله الله الله

أَلْمَنَّانُ

Al-Mannān

The Most Gracious
Exalted and Glorious

> Indeed Allāh conferred a great favor on the believers when He sent among them a Messenger from among themselves reciting unto them His verses, and purifying them, and instructing them in the Book and *al-Hikmah** while before that they had been in manifest error. (3:164)

This name is an attribute of Allāh which means the Most Gracious. Allāh shows favor to His creation and bestows benefits on them.

Anas narrated: While I was sitting with the Messenger of Allāh, may the peace and blessings be upon him, in the Mosque, a man was praying. He said during his prayer: "Oh Allāh! Behold, I ask of You because unto You belongs all praise. There is no god save You, the Most Relenting, the Most Gracious, the Originator of the heavens and the earth. Oh Lord of Majesty and Glory, Oh Living, Eternal One, of You I ask!" The Messenger of Allāh, may the peace and blessings of Allāh be upon him, said, "This man called upon Allāh by His sublimest name. When He is called upon, He responds, and when He is besought in that name He bestows." (*At-Tirmithi, Abu Dawud, Nasai' and Ibn Majah*).

الله الله الله

* the wisdom and the *sunnah* of the Prophet, may the peace and blessings of Allāh be upon him.

Al-Jalīl

The Glorious

Exalted and Glorious

Blessed be the name of your Lord (Allāh), the Owner of Majesty and Honor. (55:78)

The Messenger of Allāh, may the peace and blessings of Allāh be upon him, would say three times after completing his prayer, "I seek forgiveness of Allāh," and then he would supplicate: "Oh Allāh! You are the Peace and from You is peace. Blessed are You, Oh Lord of Majesty and Glory."

Reciting this Sacred name of Allāh is a great blessing.

Al-Jalīl is the Majestic. He is the Absolutely Great Who has perfect attributes and qualities in their perfection. He is exalted above any deficiency. So believe and know and realize that majesty and perfection belong only to your Creator.

الله الله الله

Al-Muḥiyy

The Giver of Life
Exalted and Glorious

Look then at the effects of Allāh's mercy: how He revives the earth after its death. Verily, that Allāh shall indeed raise the dead, and He is able to do all things. (30:50)

This name is an attribute of Allāh which means the Giver of Life. Every human being has been created from a dead sperm drop. This process of the dead coming to life is done by Allāh's will and grace. If a believer suffering from a chronic illness recites this name 68 times after each prayer, he may be restored to health.

Al-Muḥiyy is the Giver of Life, He Who creates life and gives it to whomever He wishes. He gives life from non-existence, and then gives them life after death. So prepare yourself for Allāh, so that He can give real life to your heart through your trust, and real life to your trust through surrender.

الله الله الله

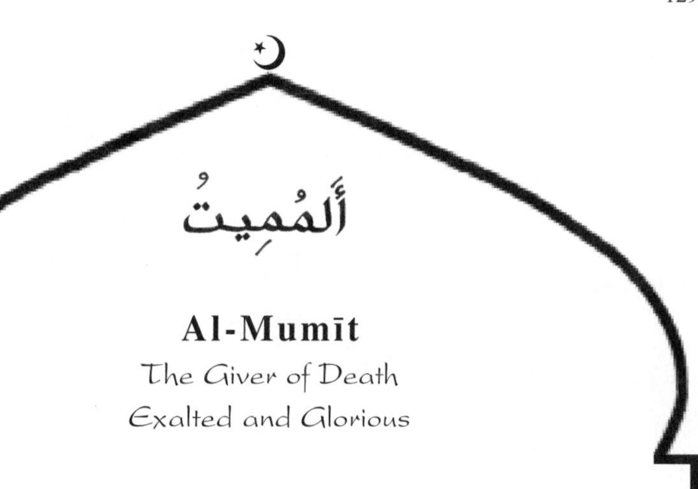

Al-Mumīt

The Giver of Death
Exalted and Glorious

Lā ᵓilāhaᵓilla ḥuwa (none has the right to be worshiped but He). It is He Who gives life and causes death. (7:158)

This name is an attribute of Allāh which means the Giver of Death. The mysteries of life and death are in the hands of Allāh who breathes life into the dead. Allāh is All-Powerful and He holds the Last Judgment so that every one should get his due reward and his due punishment.

Reciting this sacred name opens a way for redemption from the torture of the Hereafter.

Al-Mumīt, the Giver of Death is the Ordainer of the death of everything that is dead, and of everything that is living. He is the Vanquisher of His slaves whenever He wishes and as He wishes. Does not death remain in the hand of God? There is no one who is not submissive in front of His counting and His reckoning.

الله الله الله

Al-Wārith

The Inheritor
Exalted and Glorious

And certainly We! We it is Who give life, and who cause death, and We are the Inheritors. (15:23)

This name is an attribute of Allāh which means the Inheritor. To Allāh belongs the heritage of the heavens and the earth. Allāh is called so because all things proceed from Him and shall return into His hand.

He who recites this sacred name of Allāh becomes immune from the hardships and worries of this world and the Hereafter.

Couples who are having difficulty producing a child may conceive if they recite together, as often as they can, r*abbiy la tadharni fardan wa anta khayru-l-warithin*. My Lord, do not leave me without offspring, though You are the Best of Inheritors. (*anbiya*' 89)

Al-Wārith, the Inheritor is He Who is the continuing Subsister Who inherits all the characteristics of the Messenger of Allāh, may prayers and peace be upon him, after he is annihilated from the created world. He is the One Who inherits the earth and what it has. So know that if you are of those who have entered the Kingdom, then without doubt one day you will reach the Inheritor, praised is He.

الله الله الله

Al-Bā^{c}ith

The Awakener

Exalted and Glorious

> And surely, the Hour is coming, there is no doubt about it; and certainly, Allāh will resurrect those who are in the graves. (22:7)

This name is an attribute of Allāh. It means One Who Awakens. Allāh has also sent messengers with glad tidings and warnings. Allāh is called the Awakener because He shall indeed raise His creatures after their death.

By reciting this sacred name of Allāh one-hundred times every night before going to sleep, divine enlightenment will lead its way to your heart. If a person has been wrongly accused, reciting *Ya Bā^{c}ith* 7070 times may save him.

'Abdul Ba'ith is the one who has died before dying, and through his knowledge he is able to revive dead hearts, which have been killed by ignorance.

Al-Bā^{c}ith is the Arouser – He who will awaken the creation on the day of resurrection. He Who is the Dispatcher of His messengers to His slaves, and Who is the All-Giving to them, and the Awakener of their help. So if Allāh informs you of your arousing after your death, then act in awe of that day.

الله الله الله الله الله الله الله الله الله

Index of the 99 Names

The List

Arabic to English

English to Arabic

Ya Allāh! Ya Allāh! Ya Allāh!